The ... de:

Beyon... raphy

Peachpit
Press

The Digital SLR Guide: Beyond Point-and-Shoot Digital Photography
Jon Canfield

Peachpit Press
1249 Eighth Street
Berkeley, CA 94710
510/524-2178
800/283-9444
510/524-2221 (fax)

Find us on the Web at: www.peachpit.com
To report errors, please send a note to errata@peachpit.com

Peachpit Press is a division of Pearson Education

All photographs by Jon Canfield unless otherwise noted.

Acquisitions Editor: Pamela Pfiffner
Project Editor: Susan Rimerman
Production Editor: Lisa Brazieal
Development Editor: Corbin Collins
Tech Editor: Jeff Greene
Indexer: Karin Arrigoni
Composition: Danielle Foster
Cover Design: Mimi Heft
Cover Production: Andreas Schueller
Cover Photograph: Tamara Murray, iStockphoto.com

ISBN 0-321-49219-6

9 8 7 6 5 4 3 2 1

Printed and bound in the United States of America

Dedication

To Barbara, Evelyn, Bob, and Wayne. It's a blessing to have two wonderful sets of parents.

Acknowledgments

A book like this doesn't happen in a vacuum, with the writer just providing text and images. Compared to the work others put in, I think I'm a minor cog in the wheel. I'd like to start out by thanking a great group of people at Peachpit who are really responsible for what you hold in your hands. Acquisitions editor Pam Pfiffner took a rough idea and helped turn it into an innovative new book. And, when things were at their most hectic, there was always a call from Pam to keep me going. Corbin Collins did a fantastic job as development editor, keeping the book on track and readable. Technical editor Jeff Greene, with whom I've had the pleasure of working previously, did his usual great work to verify accuracy. Editor Susan Rimerman kept everything moving smoothly to make sure this project met the deadlines. And Nancy Davis, Lisa Brazieal, and everyone else at Peachpit, thank you for all your support and help in making this book happen.

I also had a great deal of support from others, including Sally Smith Clemens and Jennifer Colucci at Olympus, Scott Heath at Canon, John Nack at Adobe, and Teresa Weaver at Apple Computer. And a special thanks to Tony Sweet and Laurence Chen for providing some of the images used in this book.

Finally, there are friends and others who have provided feedback, encouragement, and support with my writing. Rob Sheppard, Chris Robinson, Wes Pitts, and George Schaub have all given me the opportunity to write for the best magazines in the field. In addition to being excellent photographers and writers, they are fantastic people—a rare combination. Friends like Charlotte Lowrie, Peter Burian, Ellen Anon, and Tony Chor have all let me bounce ideas off them with honest feedback. Jim Miotke at BetterPhoto.com has given me the opportunity to teach with some of the best photographers in the business, helping me learn to present information in a way that people seem to appreciate.

My family is my inspiration, always supporting my crazy schedules and bad habit of taking on too much at once. My wife Kathy, son Ken, and daughter Erin fill me with pride, while our Lab brothers, Luke and Clay, keep me entertained and always provide photo opportunities. Finally, and perhaps most importantly, I want to thank you! Thank you for picking up this book among the other options available to you and for reading my other books and articles. I hope this book exceeds your expectations.

Table of Contents

About the Author

Jon Canfield is the author of several popular photography books, including *Print Like a Pro* (Peachpit, 2005), *RAW 101: Better Images with Photoshop and Photoshop Elements* (Sybex, 2005), and *Photo Finish: The Digital Photographer's Guide to Printing, Showing, and Selling Images* (Sybex, 2004). In addition, he is a frequent contributor to *Shutterbug, PC Photo, Outdoor Photographer*, and *Digital PhotoPro*. His images have been published in numerous books and magazines, including the America 24/7 series. Jon formerly worked for Microsoft, where he helped develop such digital imaging products as Picture It! and Digital Image Pro. He is also a popular instructor at BetterPhoto.com.

Introduction

A few years ago, the cost of a digital SLR kept it out of the hands of everyone but pros or well-heeled enthusiasts. With prices dropping into the affordable range for many photographers, dSLR sales are now exploding. Most of the people that I see using a dSLR aren't doing much more than treating it as a large point-and-shoot camera—very seldom, if ever, taking the camera off Program mode. The prospect of shooting in advanced modes isn't made much easier by reading the manuals that come with most cameras.

When this book was first being planned, I looked at the other options available, and there were some good ones. What would set this one apart from the others? To start with, most of the books already available focus on either a specific camera or principals of photography. I wanted something different. Thanks to the efforts of Peachpit, what you're holding in your hands is that different book. It's really designed for those who are just getting started with a dSLR. If you haven't bought one yet, you'll find information that will help you select the right one. The bulk of the book, though, is about taking advantage of the features that a digital SLR provides over a compact digital camera (sometimes called a digicam).

Along with that information you'll find chapters devoted to helping you get the most from your images after the shoot, including how to work with raw images to get the maximum quality your new camera is capable of and performing basic Photoshop tasks.

Everything here applies to you regardless of the brand of camera you select—Canon, Nikon, Olympus, Pentax, or Sony—it's the common features that are covered here. When you're ready to go into detail for your specific camera, there are companion guides, called ShortCuts, that you can download directly from the Peachpit Bookstore at www.peachpit.com. And you can register this book at the site (www.peachpit.com/title/0321492196) and receive a bonus ShortCut from my book *Print Like a Pro: A Digital Photographer's Guide.*

Digital photography has brought new life to the photography world with the immediate feedback and control over how your photos are presented and shared. It's my hope that this book will give you a fast start to getting the most from your new camera and capturing images that you're proud to share.

I'd love to hear from you, whether it's questions or comments, or just to say hi. You can reach me through my Web site at www.joncanfield.com.

1 Digital SLR Basics

With the price of digital SLR (dSLR) cameras continually decreasing, you may be ready to make the move from your point-and-shoot camera to one that gives you many of the features that professional photographers use on a daily basis. Today's dSLR cameras are not only fully equipped but affordable as well. If you're getting serious about photography—or if you just want better pictures—then a dSLR may be right for you.

But how do you know what to look for when buying a camera? This chapter helps you decide what features are important and how to assess their value. I can't tell you every nuance about every individual camera model, however. Rather than get into specifics for each camera, I cover the main features to consider when you go shopping for your first digital SLR. Remember that the camera models mentioned in this book may vary from what's currently available. The rapidly changing market produces new cameras with head-spinning frequency. Once you've made a decision on basic features, compare current models to make your purchase.

Introducing Digital SLR Cameras

What makes a camera a digital SLR, anyway? And how is it different than a point-and-shoot camera?

If you're familiar with film cameras, then you know that SLR stands for *single lens reflex*, a system which uses mirrors and lenses to capture an image. When a photographer looks through a lens on an SLR camera, the image he sees enters the camera, hits a mirror, and then bounces through a prism onto a focusing screen. Just before the shutter is snapped, the mirror swings out of the way to expose the image onto a piece of film. With an SLR, the photographer sees exactly what the camera sees.

Digital SLRs work in the same way, although the image is captured by a digital *image sensor* instead of film. Like film, the sensor in your digital camera is sensitive to light; it records the amount of light that hits its surface when the shutter is opened. Color is achieved by a filter that's placed over each pixel on the sensor. In a digital camera, the union of pixel and its filter is called a *photosite.* **Figure 1.1** shows how a filter grid looks.

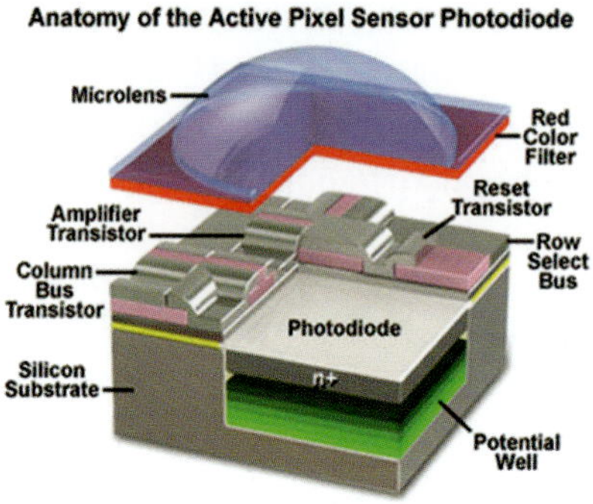

Figure 1.1 *A digital sensor is composed of millions of photosites, also called pixels, which collect light during an exposure. Circuitry then converts this light into image data that becomes a digital photo at the end of the process.*

Point-and-shoot digital cameras, also called *digicams*, are simpler in design than dSLRs, and their smaller sensors and photosites put limitations on image quality.

The most obvious distinction between the two camera types is that lenses on dSLRs are interchangeable, just like with their film cousins, whereas digicams sport a single lens that's affixed to the body. The ability to exchange lenses depending on the situation or artistic intent makes dSLR cameras much more versatile than digicams (**Figure 1.2**).

***Figure 1.2** From lightweight entry-level up to large pro-level bodies, there's a digital SLR suited for nearly every budget and need.*

One differentiating factor is becoming increasingly important: the ability to shoot in the *raw* format (see Chapter 7). Point-and-shoot cameras only produce JPEG images, which go through some processing and compression, saving space on the memory card. Images captured in their native raw format more accurately reflect the colors we see through the lens. That's because digicams producing JPEG files have to convert image data to RGB (red/green/blue, the colors that digital images mix to produce all colors) before it can be processed with an image-editing application on the computer. The conversion process discards data, which can compromise the quality of the image. Raw images, on the other hand, retain all the image data, so the photographer has greater latitude as well as control when editing images.

When you're ready to make the leap to a digital SLR, it's time to think about which camera to buy. You'll find a huge range of options with the digital SLR market, from simple-to-use, compact camera bodies up through pro-level cameras with advanced features (and price tags to match). The first step in your journey is to decide what your budget is and what features are most important to you.

Color in Black and White

Color in a digital camera is determined by the filter. Your digital camera is shooting a grayscale image, that is, black and white mixed into shades of gray. Because of the layout of the filter on the sensor, a 6-megapixel camera is actually recording 1.5 million grayscale pixels with a red filter, 1.5 million grayscale pixels with a blue filter, and 3 million grayscale pixels with a green filter. (The human eye is more sensitive to green, so having twice the number of green filters ensures that color fidelity is more accurate.) The photosites have no "knowledge" of color. The software in the camera or the raw converter processes the data and interprets these filtered grayscale pixels to create the missing color data and render a 6-megapixel full-color image.

When the exposure is made, each photosite on the sensor records the amount of light that hits it. This value is the *luminance*, or intensity of light, and ranges from black (no light) to white (fully saturated). The number of levels of intensity between black and white make up the *dynamic range*.

The luminance is recorded as red, green, or blue, determined by the color filter at each photosite, and sent to a processor. Four photosites are needed to create the data for one pixel. These pixels are laid out as green, red, green, blue, referred to as GRGB. The conversion method takes this data and interpolates it to make its best guess at the correct color values.

Price

For most people, price is *the* most important issue when looking at a camera. Until a couple of years ago, you'd have to budget well over $1,000 to purchase a digital SLR and basic lens. Today a full-featured camera can be found for less than $600. Cameras in this entry-level category, such as the Canon EOS Digital Rebel line and the Olympus E Series, are optimized for ease of use while still giving you a number of advanced features and access to the full line of lenses.

> **Note**
>
> You'll quickly discover that the camera body is often the least expensive part of your purchase. Lenses, particularly high-quality ones, can easily exceed the price of the body. The good news is that you can use your expensive lenses on a new body if you upgrade later.

Entry-level cameras

At the entry-level end of the dSLR price scale, which I'm defining as costing $700 and less, you'll find a number of cameras, often available with a *kit lens*, which is typically a zoom lens of normal to telephoto length. These cameras are typically in the 6- to 8-megapixel range and offer a number of automatic settings designed to produce good results without having to learn and master all the manual options and controls. Although excellent images can definitely be captured with these cameras, the photographer does sacrifice a significant amount of creative control.

Common to all cameras in this range are image settings for different modes, like Sports, Portrait, Landscape, and Automatic, as you see in **Figure 1.3**.

Figure 1.3 *Most entry-level cameras offer a full set of image settings designed to help you get good results with minimal fuss.*

These entry-level cameras are all designed to be easy to use, which makes them a good transition stage from a point-and-shoot. They're commonly lightweight and fairly small—especially compared to their pro-level counterparts. At its most basic, you can turn an entry-level dSLR camera on and use it as a point-and-shoot, without knowing anything about photography, by leaving the camera on its Program (P) or Auto (A) mode for automatic shutter-speed and aperture settings. When you're ready to move beyond Program, the other mode settings common to these cameras—typically Sports, Landscape, Portrait, and Macro—will help you learn more about exposure while still getting the best possible results.

Also common to cameras in this category is built-in flash for shooting in low light. The integrated flash pops up from the camera body (**Figure 1.4**) when needed, either automatically, based on shutter speed, or manually when you want to add a bit of fill light to an image. Although not as flexible or powerful as an external flash, you can't beat the convenience of having one always available.

Figure 1.4 *Pop-up flash is standard on all entry-level and most mid-level cameras, but not the pro-level bodies.*

Entry-level dSLR cameras normally allow you to capture images at a rate of 3 frames per second, making it easier to photograph moving objects. Most have enough onboard memory to record a dozen or more images before filling the memory buffer and slowing down in order to record the images to your memory card (see the "Memory Cards" sidebar).

Mid-level or "prosumer" cameras

At the next level is the group of cameras in the sub-$2,000 range, such as the Canon EOS 30D (**Figure 1.5**) and the Nikon D200. These are full-featured bodies that offer larger *buffer* sizes. The buffer is the capacity for temporarily storing images *before* the camera has

Is It All About the Megapixel?

A few years ago, a camera with 3 or 4 *megapixels* (million pixels), would have been considered top of the line. A camera with this resolution could provide a good quality 5 x 7 print.

With every new round of cameras, the number of pixels has increased, leading consumers to believe it's all about the megapixel. After all, more pixels means more resolution, and more resolution means more detail and bigger prints right?

The problem, though, is not so much the *number* of pixels. It's the *size* of those pixels on the sensor. The sensors didn't get any larger; they just squeezed more pixels onto them, making the pixels smaller and closer together. This makes the sensor more sensitive to light and, therefore, more vulnerable to *noise* problems. A dSLR gets around this in most cases because the sensor size is so much larger than what you have in the typical digicam. A 6- to 8-megapixel dSLR is capable of high-quality prints in the 11 x 14 inches or larger range—something you couldn't do easily with a digicam.

The more megapixels listed for a dSLR indicates potentially more image detail, but unless you plan on producing oversize prints at high resolutions, anything in the 6- to 10-megapixel range should be fine.

to write them to the memory card, which creates a slight delay when taking a batch of pictures in a row. This level of camera offers a faster frame-capture rate than entry-level cameras, often around 5 images per second.

Figure 1.5 The Canon 30D is an example of the mid-level range. At less than $1,500, you get a number of enhancements over the entry-level without sacrificing ease of use.

With mid-level cameras you benefit from faster focusing, options such as *bracketing* for different f-stops or shutter speeds, and in some cases, more sensitive meters that can deal with a wider range of lighting conditions to deliver accurate results in sharpness and exposure. Most mid-level dSLR cameras also include a built-in flash and faster flash synchronization, allowing you to capture images with higher shutter-speed options.

Cameras in the mid-level range are more ruggedly built than the entry-level ones, with stronger lens mounts (usually metal rather than plastic) and more robust parts (such as sturdy shutters designed to last longer). You still have the Program mode options featured in entry-level cameras and, in some cases, there are specialty modes that go under different names, such as Picture Styles (**Figure 1.6**), for optimizing camera settings for black-and-white or sepia toning, for example.

Memory Cards

Memory cards are the digital equivalent to film, with the main difference that film is a single-use item. Once exposed, it can't be used again, except of course to produce reprints. Memory cards can be used over and over. Transfer the images to your computer, erase the card, and start all over again.

There are many types, capacities, and prices of memory cards. When buying a camera it's important to think through the price and availability of the card the camera uses. Some cards, like the Sony Memory Stick, were developed as a proprietary format usable only in Sony devices. Other types, such as CompactFlash (CF), Secure Digital (SD), and the xD-Picture Card (xD), are more widely adopted by camera manufacturers.

If you have an existing stash of media cards from a current or previous camera, it makes sense to buy a camera that uses the same media so you don't have to buy new cards.

If you are starting from scratch, consider the ease, expense, and availability of cards. The more popular types, such as CF and SD, are carried by most stores selling digital cameras plus mainstream retailers such as office-supply shops and drug stores. If you're caught in a pinch and need a new card, you don't want to find that a nearby store doesn't carry that type. Compare memory card prices, too, to make sure the type you'll need doesn't cause sticker shock each time you buy one.

Figure 1.6 *Picture Styles are a helpful feature that can quickly set your camera for special effects like black and white or sepia tones.*

Memory Cards *(continued)*
Card capacity has been steadily increasing as prices decrease. 1 to 2GB cards are now widely available and quite affordable. Check the camera's technical specifications to make sure of the type and size of cards it accepts. It's possible that the model you want to purchase can't use ultra high-capacity cards.

Many pro photographers and wedding photographers use mid-level cameras as either a primary camera or a backup to their main camera. In fact, I carry one in addition to my heavy pro-level camera and find myself using it a lot. It's lighter than my pro-level camera, less obvious when I'm out in a crowd, and the built-in flash is extremely handy.

Note
You get a complete rundown on flash use, sync speeds, and all the other magical features of flashes in Chapter 5.

Pro-level cameras

The price tag of pro-level cameras (such as the Canon shown in **Figure 1.7**) puts them out of reach of most users except professionals who make a living from their photographs. You can expect to pay between $3,500 and $8,000 or more for a manufacturer's top-of-the-line camera body. Pro-level cameras are produced adhering to precise standards and tolerances with very durable materials in order to meet the challenges of daily use in a professional environment. These camera bodies are constructed with a sturdy titanium chassis and a polycarbonate shell. They include seals around all doors, buttons, and other areas where moisture or dust could seep in and cause a problem. The circuitry features gold contacts to prevent corrosion, and the camera is inspected and tested thoroughly to ensure that it meets the strict standards demanded by professional photographers.

Figure 1.7 *At the pro level, you get speed and durability along with faster focusing and other features designed for the working pro.*

Along with superior build quality comes extra weight, though. Most of these cameras are twice as heavy as prosumer bodies. Pro-level cameras offer increased frame rates, up to 8.5 frames per second on the Canon 1D Mark IIN, and more metering options, such as adjustable spot metering, that helps refine the exposure area. (I cover metering modes in Chapter 4.) Shutter speeds increase as well, to 1/8000 of a second, which is ideal for fast-action shooting in racing and other sports. You also find buffer sizes of 20 or more images to allow long sequences of images to be captured.

The professional level is also the only place you'll find a *full-frame sensor*—a sensor that's the same dimension as a frame of 35mm film. Currently, the Canon 5D and the Canon 1Ds Mark II use full-frame sensors, and more models are expected. Some of these high-end bodies include dual memory-card slots—usually for CF and SD cards—giving you more memory options and allowing you to write different image formats to different cards.

Although built to handle the needs of a working pro, there are valid reasons for the amateur photographer to consider a pro-level camera. If you're a fan of *macro*, or close-up, photography, these cameras allow you to lock the mirror before pressing the shutter to minimize any movement that's magnified with this type of photography. You'll also find support for longer exposures (compare the slight blur of **Figure 1.8a** with the sharper **Figure 1.8b**).

Figure 1.8a *Macro photography can accentuate any movement in the camera, even the slight vibration from the mirror moving out of the way.*

Figure 1.8b *Here's the same image with mirror lock-up used to eliminate movement. Camera settings were 1/30 second at f/16.*

It may surprise you to know what you *don't* get with a pro-level camera. None of these cameras include an Automatic scene mode. You'll find Program, Aperture Priority, Shutter Priority (or Time Value), and Manual—settings that are familiar to professional photographers.

You won't find a built-in flash with pro-level bodies either, which I find disappointing. Regardless of your photography level, sometimes a built-in flash is perfect for the task at hand. Instead, photographers at this level are expected to use sophisticated (and bulky) external light units.

Image Sensors

Now that you've narrowed down your price-pain threshold, let's look at underlying technologies. The type of image sensor in your camera has great impact on the quality of the images you get. The two primary sensor types are CCD (Charge Coupled Device) and CMOS (Complementary Metal Oxide Semiconductor). CCD and CMOS differ in the ways they record and process light, but the basic layout and capture methods are similar.

CCD is the most common sensor in digicams and lower-pixel count dSLRs. It is also the less expensive of the two sensors. CMOS is used by many of the high-pixel count dSLRs from Canon, Nikon, and Kodak. **Figure 1.9** compares the two types of sensors.

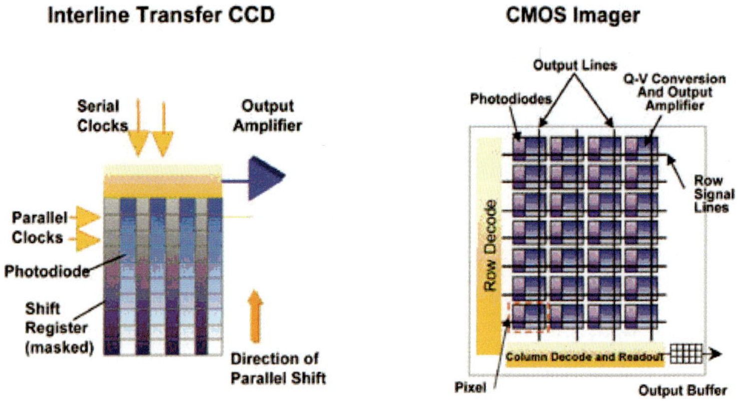

Figure 1.9 *CCD and CMOS sensors differ in how the data is processed.*

CCD and CMOS sensors are made up of *photosites*, each of which contains a *photodiode* to collect the light and convert it into electrons. The *transfer cell* collects the electrons and converts them into the digital values that make up the image. CMOS does more of the computational work at the photosite itself instead of making the transfer cell carry the load. The advantages and disadvantages to CCD and CMOS sensors are as follows:

- **Image quality.** In the beginning, the cameras that used CCD sensors had better noise-handling characteristics, which reduced the grain-like image degradation resulting from low light and high ISO speed ratings, than those using CMOS (see nearby "Noise" sidebar for more). When comparing sensors of the same size, the photodiodes on a CCD are larger and more sensitive to light, resulting in a cleaner image. However, the newest CMOS sensors have excellent built-in noise reduction that surpasses most CCD sensors. In fact, current CMOS-equipped cameras from Canon have some of the best noise-reducing characteristics of any camera available.
- **Resolution.** When compared to CCD, CMOS excels because each photosite can be read directly to the sensor, and camera makers can support multiple resolutions from the same sensor. For example, the Kodak DCS Pro SLR series cameras can record 14-megapixel, 6-megapixel, or 3-megapixel images. With a CCD-equipped camera, all 14 megapixels of information would need to be read and converted. The camera would then need to discard the excess data. This wastes processing time and battery power. CMOS, on the other hand, simply reads the required number of photosites and converts only those necessary to record the image.
- **Power consumption**. CMOS technology has the advantage of lower power consumption than CCD because most of the processing is done on the sensor itself instead of in a separate transfer cell. This reduces the power required to move and convert data. The reduction in power results in more images captured per battery charge, which translates into longer battery life.
- **Cost.** The biggest drawback to CCD sensor technology is the cost. CCD dSLR camera sensors require a large silicon-wafer footprint. CMOS, on the other hand, is less expensive to produce because it's designed to require a smaller wafer in manufacturing.

Noise

When you read reviews about digital cameras, one thing that's mentioned a lot is *digital noise*, sometimes just referred to as *noise*. It's not often though that anyone explains what noise is. If you're used to taking photos with film, you know that faster films with high ISO numbers have more *grain* because the film contains larger silver halide crystals which increase its sensitivity to light. In digital photography when you increase the ISO setting you're making the sensor more sensitive to light, just as you would by changing to a faster film. The increase in sensitivity causes more electricity to flow to each photosite which leads to the digital equivalent of grain—noise. Noise is especially problematic in dark areas of an image and with longer exposures. The good news is that you can reduce the effect of noise easily during image editing and I will show you how to do that later in the book.

How sensors work

Photosites are laid out in a grid of rows and columns as shown in **Figure 1.10**. Each photosite contains a photodiode, which collects the light as photons, and a holding cell to store that light as electrons. An exception to the typical grid is the method used by Fuji to increase the dynamic range by using *two* photodiodes for each photosite. In most cameras, a mosaic of color filters is laid over each photosite to provide color information to the image. The most common layout is the Bayer pattern, which uses twice the number of green filters as red. The filters are laid out in a green/blue row followed by red/green row, as shown in **Figure 1.11**.

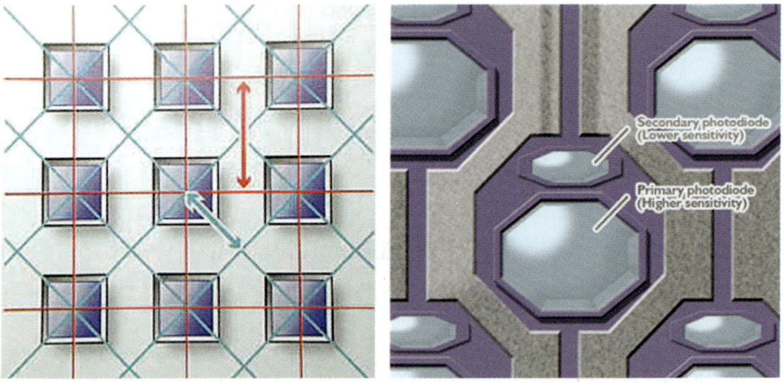

Figure 1.10 *Photosites are commonly laid out in a grid pattern on the sensor. The exception to this is the Fuji sensor which uses a honeycomb pattern with two photodiodes for each pixel to increase dynamic range.*

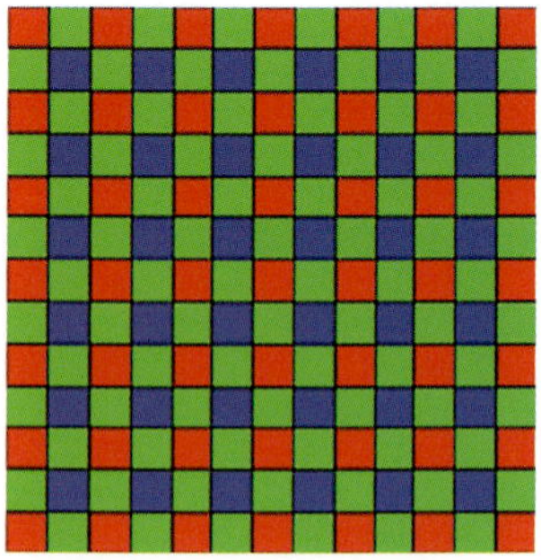

Figure 1.11 *The Bayer pattern is the most commonly used filter system in digital sensors. There are twice as many green filters as there are red or blue because the human eye is most sensitive to green.*

Although the Bayer pattern is by far the most commonly used filter array, there are other methods of recording the color values. Early CCD sensors used a three-pass system where each exposure was recorded three times—once for red, once for green, and once for blue. These separate exposures were then combined to create a single color image. This method is still used in some cameras, notably in astrophotography to record faint celestial objects while minimizing noise, as well as some large- and medium-format digital backs that attach to a conventional camera. Because three separate exposures are required to produce a single image, this type of sensor doesn't work for handheld photography. In fact, it often requires that they be connected to a computer that does the processing work of combining each of the separate exposures into one image.

Sensor and photosite size

The size of the sensor helps to determine how large the individual photosites are and how densely they are packed together. Both size of the sensor and density of the photosites play an important role in the quality of the captured image. Smaller photosites are unable to gather as much light as larger photosites before filling up. When these sites are packed closer together, the overflow can affect the light being captured by the neighboring photosites.

The majority of digicams, or point-and-shoot digital cameras, use a very small sensor that is approximately 8.8mm × 6.6mm, so image noise is frequently a problem. On the other hand, many dSLR models use a much larger sensor, measuring 23.4 × 16.7mm. Currently, only the Canon 5D and Canon 1Ds Mark II use full-frame sensors that have the same measurements as a frame of 35mm film: 24mm × 36mm. This larger sensor size allows lenses to be used with no extra magnification and also provides higher-resolution image files with larger photosites, thus producing a higher-quality image. **Figure 1.12** shows the relative size of each of these sensors compared to a 35mm negative.

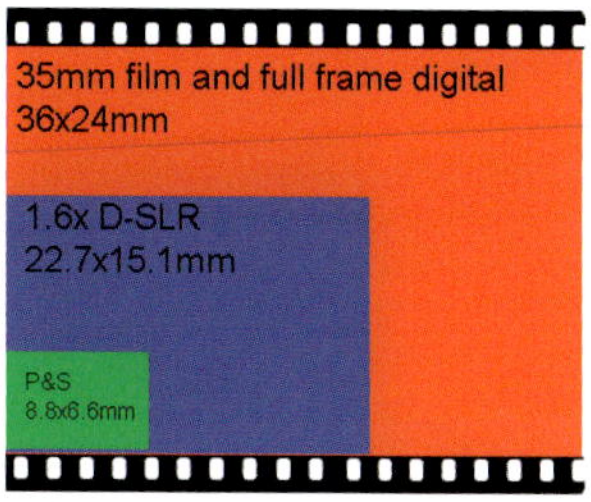

Figure 1.12 *Most sensors are smaller than conventional 35mm film. The larger the sensor, the more detail it can capture. As you can see from this example, digital SLRs have a significant advantage over the digicam in sensor size.*

However, the single most important determination in image quality is the size of the individual photosites. Smaller photosites are unable to handle as much light before they spill over. This overfill is most commonly seen as *blooming*, which shows up in a digital image as a white glow that looks like a slight halo, as shown in **Figure 1.13**. This is not the same thing as *chromatic aberration*, which is seen as color fringing around areas with strong lighting, although the two effects are related in cause. You are most likely to see blooming and chromatic aberration when transitioning from strong light to dark areas, such as leaves against a bright sky. Because smaller photosites fill more quickly, they also have lower dynamic range—there are fewer levels of light held before the photosite is saturated to full white. Although it's always best to choose a camera that minimizes these artifacts, I discuss later how to correct some of them in Adobe Photoshop.

Figure 1.13 *Blooming and chromatic aberration occurs when a photosite is flooded with more light than it can handle. Here you can see blooming on the chrome area (if you take your eyes off the cute doggie).*

Figure 1.14 shows the difference between two cameras with the same resolution but different sensor sizes. The image on the left was taken with a digicam using the small sensor typical in these models. The image on the right was taken with a dSLR with a much larger sensor. The dSLR image is more resolute, has better color rendition, and contains smoother transitions along the edges where the tonality changes.

Figure 1.14 *The image on the right was captured with a digital SLR using a large sensor, and the left-hand image was captured with a compact camera and the typical small sensor size. As you can see, the digital SLR has captured much more detail thanks in large part to the larger photosites.*

Camera Features

Once you've decided on the price range and image sensor type that fits your budget, it's time to look at other features. Although every camera shares some common characteristics, each company adds its own unique touch to the cameras it sells.

Every dSLR camera, regardless of cost or skill level, includes at a minimum the major shooting modes:

- Aperture Priority lets you control the aperture (and thus depth of field) while the camera selects the appropriate shutter speed.
- Shutter Priority (or Time Value) lets you set the shutter speed while the camera selects the aperture.
- Program chooses both shutter and aperture for you.

dSLR cameras also include a Manual mode in which you control both shutter speed and aperture. By utilizing the built-in meter, an accurate combination of shutter speed and aperture can be applied to capture a properly exposed image, just as in 35mm SLR film cameras.

You should also be able to choose between manual focus and auto-focus, and every dSLR I've come across lets you choose whether you want continuous auto-focus for tracking moving subjects or single auto-focus for stationary subjects.

Finally, you have a choice of metering modes. All cameras have some form of *matrix* metering, where the entire scene is evaluated by the camera's meter and averaged for the best exposure, and a *center-weighted* metering mode, where just the central portion of the image is considered for exposure. I cover metering modes in Chapter 4.

For example, some cameras have an anti-shake feature that minimizes vibration, especially at slower shutter speeds, resulting in sharper images. Canon and Nikon both offer anti-shake with some of their lenses (see Chapter 3). Pentax and Sony build the stabilization into the camera body itself, so any lens you use is stabilized.

Get ready for the wonderful world of dust. Compact cameras don't have this problem because you never remove the lens and the system remains sealed from outside elements. With a dSLR, however, every time you change lenses you expose the sensor to dust in the air. And, because a sensor is electrically charged, it acts like a magnet. You'll know that you have dust on your sensor when you see spots in your photos (**Figure 1.15**) that remain constant from one image to the next. In Chapter 8 you learn how to use an image-editing program to remove dust from your photos.

A couple of manufacturers incorporate dust removal into the camera itself. The Olympus E Series has a "Supersonic Wave Filter" which vibrates the sensor briefly on start-up to shake any dust off the sensor before you start your photographic session.

Figure 1.15 *Dust on the sensor can be a problem for most cameras. Olympus uses a special filter to remove dust when you turn the camera on.*

Lens selection

Owners of Canon EOS and Nikon film SLR cameras will be happy to know that your existing lenses will work with the new digital body, making your purchase decision that much easier. If you're just getting into SLR photography, the types of lenses available for the camera body should be high on your list of priorities when you select a body.

Almost all dSLR cameras are sold as a kit that includes the camera body and a default lens. Most lenses chosen by the manufacturer are zoom lenses and address a wide range of situations from regular portrait or scene photography to adequate telephoto uses. These lenses are absolutely fine, but you may want to explore other options.

The type of photography you are interested in will drive your lens choice. Landscape photography fans will want to look into a system with good wide-angle lenses, while the wildlife fan is going to want a selection of telephoto lenses to get closer to elusive subjects. The nuances of these specialty lenses vary (see Chapter 3).

A final consideration with lens selection is the availability of third-party lenses such as those from Sigma, Tamron, and Tokina. These companies make lenses for Canon and Nikon as well as for Olympus, Pentax, and Sony. But you'll find the widest selection of lenses for Canon and Nikon brands.

If your interests include underwater photography, housings are available for Nikon and Canon, along with special flash units designed to be used underwater. For small, detailed subject matter, Olympus, Nikon, and Canon all offer special flash units for macro photography (**Figure 1.16**).

Figure 1.16 *Special flash units are available from some companies. This flash, from Canon, is designed to be used for macro photography.*

Deciphering a Data Sheet

When you shop for a dSLR, you'll find a bewildering array of options. Salespeople will hand you data sheets that describe in sometimes painful detail what the camera can do. In this section, I explain the major areas to look for when you go shopping for that first dSLR. By the way, this book's Glossary is another source of information for unfamiliar terms.

Recording medium

The recording medium is the type of memory card used by the camera, such as CF (Compact Flash) memory cards. The most common card is Type I (3.3mm thick), whereas some, such as the MicroDrive, are Type II (5mm thick). Devices equipped with Type II slots can also accept Type I cards, but not vice-versa. Other common types of memory cards used in dSLRs are SD (Secure Digital) and xD Picture Cards (see "Memory Cards" sidebar earlier in this chapter).

Aspect ratio

The 3:2 aspect (width to height) ratio is the most common for digital photographs and is the same ratio that a traditional 35mm film camera uses. Other available ratios you'll find are 4:3 and 16:9.

Color filter system

Most dSLR image sensors use an RGB filter to record a single color on each photosensor to produce an accurate image. The exception is the Foveon X3 sensor which uses a color-separation beam-splitter prism assembly and utilizes all the light and records all colors at all locations on the sensor. This technology is currently featured in the Sigma line of dSLR cameras.

Recording and image format

A dSLR should take and store photos in both JPEG and raw formats. This means that images are written to the memory card in a way that can be understood by image-editing programs. Although JPEG is a widely accepted format in virtually every software application, raw files are proprietary to each individual manufacturer and require their software, or a licensed third-party application, to convert to an editable file.

File size

Most cameras support saving JPEG files in various sizes up to a limit, normally given as maximum file size. This is the recommended manner for capture to ensure the best quality enlargements. Shooting smaller files is quicker, allows more images to be stored on a card, and is ideal for Web use.

Image-processing parameters

Some cameras enable you to create preset custom settings that can be quickly recalled for shooting specific situations, eliminating the need to select each individual setting from the menus every time you want to use them.

Interface

The interface is how the camera is connected to your computer. You'll find either USB 2.0 or FireWire (IEEE 1394) as options. Be sure your computer has a FireWire port if you choose a camera with a FireWire interface.

White balance

With most dSLRs, the white balance, measured in degrees Kelvin, can be set for the appropriate light source. Presets for daylight, shade, cloudy, tungsten, fluorescent, and flash are common options. All digital cameras also provide an Auto preset where the camera can more accurately determine the proper white balance based on the current light source. Finally, most cameras also let you create a custom setting for a mixed light source or specific lighting situation, such as in a studio.

Viewfinder coverage

Most viewfinders don't show you the entire image being captured. More expensive pro-level dSLRs often have 100-percent viewfinder coverage. This is a tremendous advantage for properly evaluating composition and framing.

Magnification

The magnification level in the viewfinder relates to how large the scene appears when you look through the eyepiece. A magnification of .8x is considered very good.

Viewfinder information

This is a listing of all the information that can be displayed in the viewfinder around the frame. Thankfully, you'll never see all of it at once. Chapter 4 has more details on reading the information in your viewfinder.

Depth-of-field preview

Landscape and macro photographers in particular find a depth-of-field preview very helpful. This works by closing the aperture down to the selected setting to let you see what areas of your scene are in focus before you take the shot.

Eyepiece shutter

For long exposures, it's helpful to cover the eyepiece to keep stray light from entering. Some pro cameras have a built-in shutter, and others come with a simple cover you can snap on.

ISO speed range

The speed range refers to the different range of ISO (International Organization for Standardization) film speed settings you can use. Many dSLR cameras can go as high as ISO 3200. Remember though, just as in 35mm photography, the higher the ISO setting, the more noise (graininess) issues you'll have with the image. You can use higher ISO settings in lower light situations to increase the sensitivity of the sensor just as you would by using faster film with a traditional camera. I cover ISO in more detail in Chapter 2.

Exposure compensation

Exposure compensation, in the form of f-stops, adjusts the camera to automatically add or subtract some light from the exposure setting you're using. This is useful when shooting very bright, backlit subjects or very dark scenes. Essentially, it instructs the camera to overexpose or underexpose an image based on what the camera would incorrectly perceive as the correct exposure setting. Bracketing is a feature that enables the camera to take a set of images, usually three, with different settings to increase the chances of capturing one correctly exposed image.

Noise reduction for long exposure

Built-in noise reduction works by taking a second image without opening the shutter. This is called the *dark*. The camera then compares the dark and the real image, and wherever there are matching pixels, or noise, they are removed and replaced with dark pixels.

2 Mastering Digital SLR Controls

It might surprise you to know that digital SLRs share many of the same features as their compact digicam cousins, but in an odd twist of irony, it's often easier to access most of the controls on a digital SLR than on a compact camera. Where the digicams tend to force you to go through multiple levels of menus on the LCD screen to get to settings such as ISO, aperture, and shutter speed, the SLR has quick access via buttons or dials to let you make changes while you shoot without distraction.

In this chapter, I will show you the common controls that you'll find on most digital SLRs, with special attention to the controls you'll find yourself accessing frequently.

Using Program Mode

Figure 2.1 *The Setting dial on a typical digital SLR, with Program, Aperture, Shutter, Manual, and Scene mode settings.*

The first stop for almost everyone is Program mode. Usually identified with a P (**Figure 2.1**), this mode puts all control in the hands of the camera. Both aperture and shutter speed are set automatically, based on how the camera senses the available light, which lets you concentrate on learning how to compose and focus—ideal for someone just moving into a full-featured camera.

Letting the camera choose

Program mode is often the easiest way to get used to a new camera, allowing you to concentrate on focusing, metering, composition, and just capturing images.

You'll find Program mode useful when your camera supports automatic flash settings as well. The camera, in addition to setting the shutter speed and aperture, automatically determines the proper output from the external flash to give you the extra light needed for a successful image. Note that this is not true in Canon dSLR cameras.

With Canons, the flash only pops up automatically in scene modes such as Auto (green square), Portrait, Macro, and Night mode.

Program Shift modes

Even with Program mode selected, most cameras include a feature known as Program Shift or Shiftable Program. In this mode, you can control either the shutter speed or aperture, and the camera adjusts the other setting to keep the exposure consistent. Although this sounds very similar to Aperture Priority and Shutter Priority modes, the difference is that once you capture the image in Program Shift mode, the camera resets back to the default Program mode settings.

Figure 2.2 *Scene modes are simply presets designed to optimize the camera settings for different types of photography.*

Scene modes

Common to many entry- and mid-level digital SLRs are Scene modes (**Figure 2.2**). These settings, often symbolized by tiny graphics, are optimized for each type of image capture to set the aperture or shutter speed for the best results.

- **Landscape mode** is designed to give you the most depth of field, or range of focus, which is typically what you want when shooting landscape-type images with everything from near to far in focus (**Figure 2.3**).

Note

There is nothing in these Scene modes that you can't do easily on your own. Modes do make it easier, though, by automatically setting the optimum shutter speed or aperture especially while you're learning about photography and your camera.

Figure 2.3 *Landscape mode maximizes depth of field.*

- **Sport mode** is optimized for fast shutter speed, sacrificing depth of field in order to freeze action. Because of this, focusing on your subject is critical in order to have the proper focus point (**Figure 2.4**).

Figure 2.4 *Sport mode optimizes shutter speed for moving subjects.*

- **Portrait mode** uses a shallow depth of field to keep the background areas out of focus when photographing people. This helps isolate the subject from the background (**Figure 2.5**). In some cameras, this mode also activates the built-in flash to give fill light to the subject.

Figure 2.5 *Portrait mode uses a shallow depth of field to blur backgrounds.*

- **Macro mode** maximizes depth of field at the expense of shutter speed. Because of the close distances used for macro photography, depth of field is always a problem, so this setting usually chooses an aperture of f/16 or smaller if available (**Figure 2.6**). To get the best results, use a tripod for this type of work.

Figure 2.6 *Macro mode maximizes depth of field even more than Landscape mode and is best for working with close-up subjects.*

- **Backlight mode** forces the use of the built-in flash to compensate for heavy shadows and lighting conditions that would result in your subject being underexposed (**Figure 2.7**).

Figure 2.7 *Backlight mode forces the built-in flash to be used to avoid heavy shadows and underexposure even when shooting into bright light.*

- **Backlight mode** is also good for scenes where you want to force the flash to fire regardless of the light.

Using Aperture Settings

Aperture Priority, sometimes referred to as AV or Aperture Value, is used when you need to control which parts of your image are in focus. Landscape and portrait photography are almost exclusively shot with Aperture Priority and for exactly the same reason, even though the desired results are polar opposites.

Aperture and f-stop basics

Aperture controls depth of field in your images by changing the size of the diaphragm in the lens to control light. Smaller numbers, like 4.0, 3.5, and 2.8, mean a larger opening (**Figure 2.8**) which allows more light to hit the sensor in less time. This also gives you less depth of field, or range of focus.

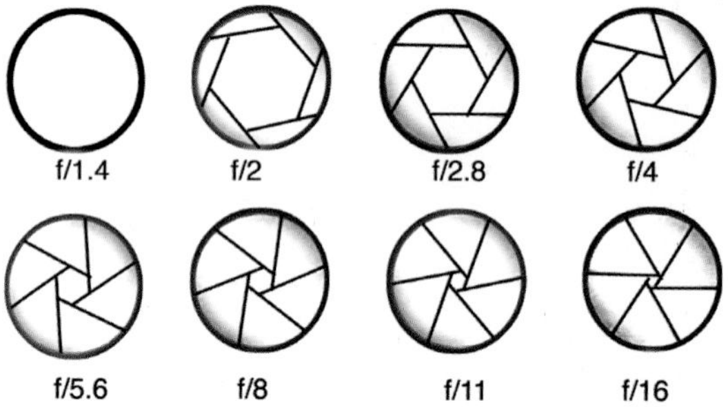

Figure 2.8 *The diaphragm in a lens controls the amount of light passing through to the sensor. Larger openings give shorter exposures and less depth of field.*

Each change in aperture, or *f-stop*, doubles or halves the exposure time, depending on whether the number goes up or down. As you go up in aperture and close the diaphragm, you reduce the amount of light hitting the sensor, and the shutter compensates by leaving the shutter open longer so that roughly the same amount of light ends up hitting the sensor. As an example, if a setting of f/4 gives you an exposure of 1/60 second, changing to f/5.6, the next higher f-stop, doubles the exposure time to 1/30 second. Going the other direction, lowering the f-stop to f/2.8 cuts the exposure time in half, to 1/125 second.

Controlling depth of field

Let's take a look at some real examples of how aperture settings affect depth of field. In the example shown in **Figure 2.9**, the lens is set to f/2.8, which gives a narrow depth of field but fast shutter speed.

Figure 2.9 *This image was captured at f/2.8 with a very shallow depth of field.*

Moving the aperture setting to f/8, or three stops, puts more of the image in focus (**Figure 2.10**). A setting in this range is a good compromise between depth of field and shutter speed, especially when there is movement in the image.

Figure 2.10 *By adjusting the aperture to f/8, more of the image is in focus.*

Finally, by using an aperture setting of f/22, an additional three stops, we've maximized the depth of field to get as much of the image in focus as possible (**Figure 2.11**), but must now accept a very slow shutter speed to accommodate such a small aperture. This is also ideal for a landscape image where you have detail in the foreground and in the distance that are both important to the image.

Figure 2.11 *An aperture of f/22 maximizes the area that is in sharp focus.*

Another time you use aperture settings creatively is to control exposure time for things such as moving water, where you want that silky smooth look (**Figure 2.12**). Although you can accomplish the same thing with a Shutter Priority mode setting, it's often quicker to adjust the aperture in the current mode. Doing so changes the shutter speed automatically until it reaches your desired setting, all without taking your eye from the viewfinder.

Figure 2.12 You can also use aperture to slow down the exposure and create movement.

For **Figure 2.12**, I used an aperture of f/18 to give me a slow enough shutter speed to blur the waterfall, but still keep the kayak as sharp as possible. Needless to say, when using slow shutter speeds a tripod is mandatory to ensure overall image sharpness.

Using Shutter Speed Settings

Shutter Priority, also known as Time Value or TV on some cameras, is the best choice when you want to control how long of an exposure you take and don't care as much about the depth of field. An example of this type of image capture is sports photography, where you really want to freeze the subject in motion. Another is where the wind is blowing, and you want to avoid the blurring of trees, flowers, and grasses.

Freezing motion

Whether you're shooting fast-moving cars, athletes, or kids and dogs, stopping the action can make the difference between a successful sharp image and one that appears unsharp due to unwanted motion blur (**Figure 2.13**). In these situations, a fast shutter speed is required to stop the action and provide sharp detail in the main subject.

Figure 2.13 *Too slow of a shutter speed can ruin an image with a moving subject.*

Unless you're using flash, as a rule a good minimum shutter speed when photographing people is 1/125. When the subject isn't moving quickly, such as the figure skaters shown in **Figure 2.14**, 1/60 is often enough to capture a sharp image. Flash helps to freeze action much better and is typically used at shutter speeds of 1/60 to 1/250 (or higher), depending on the camera.

Figure 2.14 *A shutter speed of 1/60 is enough to freeze the movement of these skaters when they aren't moving much.*

Faster-moving subjects like cars often need a faster shutter speed, or they require you to use creative techniques at slower speeds, which I cover a bit later. To freeze a car moving at freeway speeds, a shutter speed of 1/250 should be considered a minimum (**Figure 2.15**).

Figure 2.15 *A car on the freeway is in sharp focus when shot at 1/250.*

Shutter speed also changes with distance. The closer a moving subject is to the camera, the faster shutter speed you need to capture the image. As an example, the image shown in **Figure 2.16** was shot at 1/180, even though the planes are going several hundred miles per hour. Had they been closer and filling more of the frame, I would have needed a shutter speed of 1/2000 to freeze the action.

Figure 2.16 *Even though these jets are moving at hundreds of miles an hour, they are far enough away that a fast shutter speed isn't required.*

Emphasizing motion

Sometimes freezing the action is exactly the wrong thing to do. For instance, flowing water like that shown in **Figure 2.17** takes on a silky, smooth look thanks to a slow shutter speed of one second.

Figure 2.17 *A one-second exposure has turned this waterfall into a smooth blur.*

This technique is also good to show some movement and action in a photo to emphasize the activity. In **Figure 2.18** the same 1/60 exposure used in the earlier example (**Figure 2.14**, in which they were not moving so fast) of the ice skaters now shows the skater in a fast spin, letting the viewer see the speed at which the subject is moving. Again, a sturdy tripod is essential to retain sharpness in stationary objects within the image.

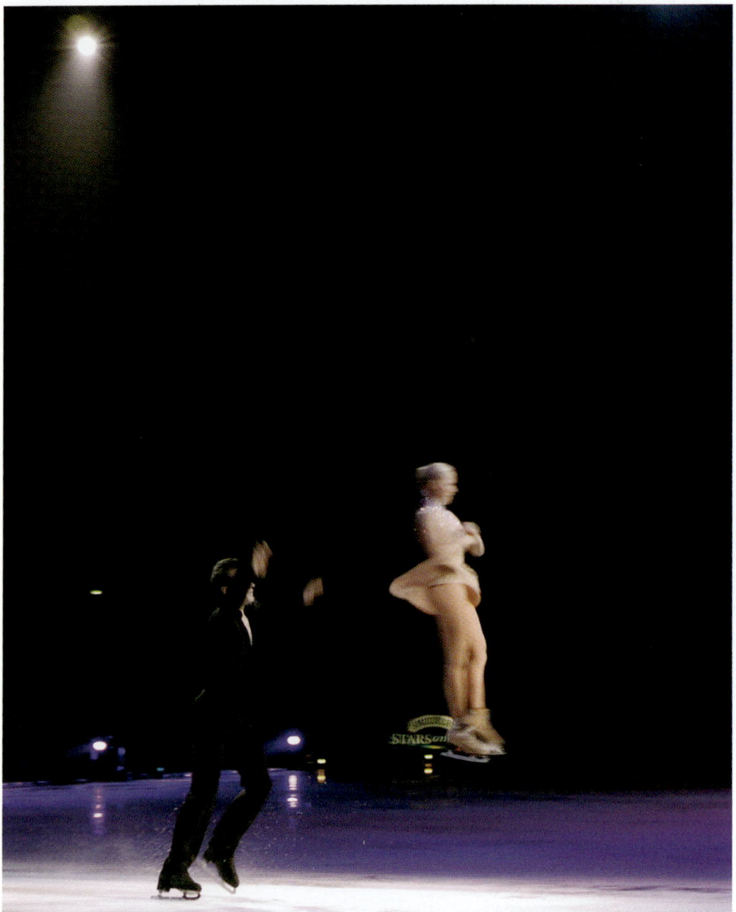

Figure 2.18 *Using the same 1/60 exposure as Figure 2.14, movement now produces motion blur.*

Creative techniques

Combining motion and sharp detail can make for very compelling images, especially when shooting fast visual spectacles such as sports. The technique of *panning* is one of the few times when you intentionally move the camera while shooting. In **Figure 2.19**, the camera moved along with the motorcyle while pressing the shutter button. This provided a sharp image of the motorcyclist with a nicely blurred background to really show the speed.

PHOTO BY LAURENCE CHEN

Figure 2.19 *Panning the camera with the movement of your subject is an effective method of showing action while keeping your subject in focus.*

Another use of slower shutter speeds and movement is shown in **Figure 2.20**. Here I twisted the camera during a long exposure of a 1/2 second at f/32 to give an ordinary photo of tulips an abstract look.

Figure 2.20 *Intentionally moving the camera during an exposure can produce interesting effects.*

You can do something similar by moving the zoom lens in or out during a long exposure (**Figure 2.21**), adding an explosive look to the image. This works best with bright colors that pull the viewer's eye into the photo.

Figure 2.21 *Zooming in or out during exposure is another fun technique to experiment with.*

Choosing ISO Settings

If you're used to shooting with a compact digital camera, you've probably learned to stay away from anything but the lowest ISO settings, such as 100 or 200, because of noise problems associated with more light-sensitive ratings of 400 or higher.

Luckily, digital SLRs are much better in this regard, and images shot at ISO settings of 400 and as high as 1600 are very usable. Why would you want to use these higher settings? There are two main reasons. The first is to give you more exposure options in low-light conditions, and the second is for creative techniques.

ISO basics

Most digital SLRs have a low-end ISO setting of 100 or 200, and the image quality is optimized for these settings. You see the least amount of noise when shooting at these settings because there is less of an electrical charge going to the sensor to capture the image than there would be at a higher ISO. This is a result of the increased heat and electrical activity required of the sensor to record the image data. Under normal lighting conditions and when using a flash, this is all fine. But when the light starts to fade, at low ISOs you find that you either can't get an exposure reading at all or the exposure (shutter speed) must be so slow that a sharp image isn't possible without a tripod. This is particularly problematic with low-end zoom lenses with small maximum apertures that come with many entry-level digital SLRs.

In cases like this, it's time to increase the ISO setting of your camera. Like changing the exposure by adjusting the aperture or shutter speed, increasing the ISO works to add (or subtract) light to the image. It works a bit differently though—rather than changing the depth of field, or the amount of time the shutter is open, increasing the ISO changes how sensitive the sensor is to the light that hits it during the exposure. Going from ISO 200 to ISO 400 doubles the sensor's sensitivity and gives you an additional stop of exposure latitude. In other words, if you have an exposure of 1/30 at f/5.6

with an ISO of 200, by changing to ISO 400 your new exposure will be 1/60 at f/5.6 or 1/30 at f/8. However, the downside is that the increased sensor sensitivity also increases noise, or grain, in the image. The image degradation caused by noise increases proportionally with each increase in ISO sensitivity.

High ISO techniques

It might sound strange, but there are times when a high ISO setting is used intentionally to *add* noise, or grain, to the image. This is particularly useful when capturing black-and-white images in which you want to have an old-ish film look (**Figure 2.22**) that simulates grain.

Figure 2.22 *High ISO settings can be used to give a grainy look to images.*

In the examples shown in **Figure 2.23** and **2.24**, I increased the speed to ISO 1250 to make the sensor much more sensitive to light, thus producing noise. As a color image it looks noisy (**Figure 2.23**), but after converting it to black and white (**Figure 2.24**) in Photoshop and giving it an edge treatment, it has a very effective vintage look that would have been more difficult to achieve without the added noise.

Figure 2.23 In color, the noise doesn't work to this photo's advantage.

Figure 2.24 After converting to black and white and adding a vintage border, the noise from shooting at high ISO looks like it belongs.

Image Capture Options

Many advanced compact cameras support raw image capture, but few are optimized for it (see Chapter 7 for much more on raw image capture). All digital SLRs support raw, and many are capable of recording images in raw and JPEG at the same time. Which format is best?

Raw capture

For pure image quality, you can't beat raw. The raw format is simply a recording of the light values as seen by each pixel when the image is captured on the camera sensor. There are no modifications made to the data, and it's stored in the full bit depth supported by the camera (typically 12 bits) for the maximum color information.

So why wouldn't you use raw? Well, although it gives you the best image quality, it also takes some extra effort on your part to achieve those results. You can't just take a raw file from your camera and print a photo. There is some pre-processing required first to render the unprocessed sensor data to a useable file format, such as a JPEG or TIFF, for editing, enhancement, and printing. If you're doing hundreds of photos for, let's say, a kid's soccer event, you very likely do not want to spend the time needed to process all these images. In cases like this, it makes more sense to shoot in JPEG, which, when accurately exposed in-camera, I consider to be "good enough" much of the time.

When you're ready to explore what the raw format has to offer, see Chapter 7, which goes into much more detail on raw formats and using the image-conversion software that it requires.

JPEG settings

JPEG is the most useable file format around for photos. Every online photo lab, Wal-Mart, kiosk, and other photo-printing location supports JPEG photos directly. If your images are taken in JPEG, then you can take the memory card out of your camera, pop it into their machine, and it spits out all the photos you want with minimal fuss or effort.

So, why *wouldn't* you use JPEG? The biggest reason is image quality. When you shoot with JPEG, you start out by throwing away image information. dSLR cameras, in raw mode, are capable of recording in 12-bit (128 tonal values) color; that's 4,096 color values per pixel. Shooting in JPEG mode reduces that to 8-bit color (28 tonal values), or 256 color values per pixel. JPEG also compresses your images. In theory, this sounds great. After all, you can store more images on a memory card and print them at a nearby store. But in order to compress those images, additional information is thrown away, which reduces the quality of the image. So, it's a trade-off.

Finally, JPEG is a processed file. When you capture an image in your camera, it is first captured as a raw image, no matter which format you're shooting. But if you store them as JPEG, for every image the camera automatically takes the raw file, applies image settings such as white balance, saturation, sharpening, and compression, and then converts that to the JPEG format before storing it on the memory card. The biggest drawback to this process is the lack of control you have over the final product. When capturing in JPEG, you're trusting the camera to choose the right settings for optimizing the image. For example, if you have the incorrect white balance set on the camera, the image is processed with an inaccurate color shift and saved. With raw, you can set the white balance to any value since it is not saved as a separate image until the raw file is processed and saved into an editable format such as a JPEG, TIFF, or PSD file.

Note

If you do plan to shoot in JPEG, you have the option to select a quality level. I highly recommend that you use the highest quality level setting to retain as much information as possible. After all, you spent a good chunk of money to improve your photos, so why save them at anything less than the best possible quality?

Focus Modes

Another major area of difference between a compact digicam and a digital SLR is in the ability to select focus modes. Whereas a compact camera focuses on a subject and then captures the image, a dSLR can easily shoot in Continuous Focus mode, tracking a moving subject and keeping it in focus until, and even after, you press the shutter button.

Continuous Focus

Continuous Focus, sometimes called Servo, or AI, or Predictive Auto Focus, is designed for sports and wildlife photography where the subject is moving and the photographer is panning the camera along with the subject prior to capturing the image. This mode works on most cameras by pressing the shutter button halfway to activate the metering and focus tracking. (Some cameras have alternative ways to activate focus.) Depending on your camera, one or more focus points (**Figure 2.25**) will lock onto the subject, and as it moves the lens will change focus to keep the subject sharp.

When you're ready to capture the image, press the shutter the rest of the way down. You need to be careful when using Continuous Focus mode. It's entirely possible and all too easy to end up with photos that are out of focus and blurry (trust me, I have hundreds of examples). Unless your subject is moving, I suggest you use Single Shot Focus mode (see the next section), which requires your camera to be in focus before taking the photo.

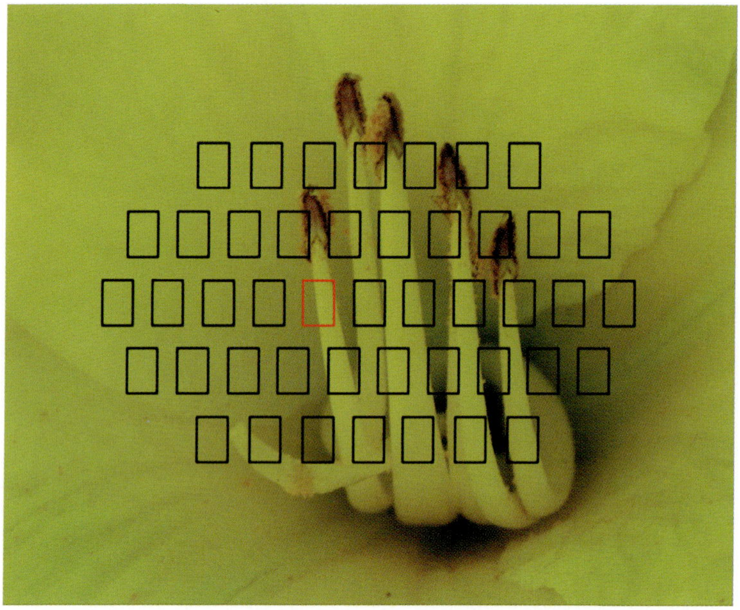

Figure 2.25 *Most digital SLRs have multiple focus points to select from.*

Single Shot Focus

As its name suggests, Single Shot Focus mode locks onto a focus point as the shutter button is pressed and then stays there. Unlike Continuous Focus Mode, which locks into, follows, and maintains focus on a moving subject, Single Shot Focus mode doesn't release the shutter until the camera has focused on the subject. Once you've locked focus on the subject, you can then press the shutter button halfway and recompose the scene, repositioning the subject in another part of the frame. As long as the shutter remains pressed halfway, and the subject hasn't moved, it will remain in focus.

3 Selecting and Using Lenses

Lens selection is one of the most obvious differences between a digicam (a compact digital camera) and a dSLR. The choice of available SLR lenses is extensive, ranging from wide-angle and fisheye lenses up through super telephoto lenses. And along with the wide choice of these different focal lengths, you'll find an even larger range in prices, depending on lens quality and features.

In this chapter, I cover the different lens types available and give examples of the types of photos you can capture with each. Lenses are broken down into zoom, wide-angle, standard, and telephoto focal lengths, and there is also a section on specialty lenses.

Lens Basics

Modern lenses are complex creations with specialized coatings on the glass to optimize color quality and image sharpness. **Figure 3.1** shows a cross-section illustration of a zoom lens. As you can see, multiple lens elements make up a modern lens.

These lens elements direct the light coming into the lens to create an image on the sensor in your camera. Early lenses, and many of the less expensive lenses available today, have no coatings on the lens elements, which causes the light to scatter as it travels through the lens to the sensor, resulting in images that look soft or have color problems called *chromatic aberration*. In the past, many pros avoided zoom lenses in favor of fixed-length, or *prime*, lenses to avoid these issues. In recent years, though, the quality of zoom lenses has improved greatly to the point where many of the better zooms on the market now rival the prime lenses they compete against.

The other major component of a lens is the *diaphragm*, which is the iris-type opening at the camera end of a lens. By changing the size of the opening in the diaphragm, you control how much light enters the lens, and therefore how much *depth of field*, or area of focus, is captured. The size of the opening is the *aperture* of the lens.

When you start to examine the variety of lenses available on the market, you find two things very quickly. First, there's a wide range of focal lengths, or lens sizes, available for most dSLR cameras. Second, you could easily mortgage your house to purchase some of these lenses. Fast lenses—those with large maximum apertures of f/2.8 or f/4—and telephoto lenses can be extremely expensive and heavy to boot. As an example, the Canon EF 500 IS f4L lens, a very popular option with wildlife photographers (**Figure 3.2** was shot with it), weighs in at a healthy 8.5 pounds, and costs a wallet-draining $5,500.

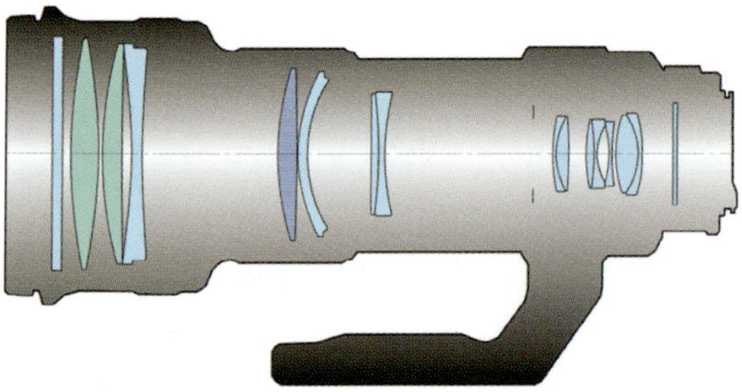

Figure 3.1 *As you can see from this illustration, a modern lens is a complex piece of equipment with many glass elements. Image courtesy Canon USA.*

Figure 3.2 *The Canon EF 500 IS f4L is a popular choice among wildlife shooters, but it's a heavy and expensive lens, partially because of the faster aperture.*

Zoom Lenses

Zoom lenses are a popular compromise for many users. The advantages are obvious—you get the equivalent of many different focal lengths all in one compact package. Most "kit lenses," or those that come with a digital SLR, are zoom lenses that cover the wide-angle to telephoto range (**Figure 3.3**)

Figure 3.3 *A typical kit lens will give you the equivalent of a 28-90 mm zoom. These lenses are usually not the best optical lenses, but they are a good starting point if you're just getting into dSLR photography.*

The most common zooms cover the 35mm film equivalent of 28mm to 90mm focal-length lenses, and often have a variable maximum aperture, which keeps the cost and size of the lens down. An example of this is the standard lens included with the Canon Digital Rebel. This zoom lens has a focal length that ranges from 18-55mm with a maximum aperture that varies from f/3.5-5.6. In lay terms, the lens has a maximum aperture of f/3.5 when set to 18mm, and f/5.6 when zoomed out to 55mm. Because the Digital Rebel's sensor is smaller than the traditional 24mm x 36mm film frame, it has a *magnification factor* of 1.6x. Therefore this lens would be equivalent to a 28-90mm lens on a standard 35mm camera. The focal length is different, but the aperture doesn't change. A professional-quality zoom lens with a constant aperture setting

Digital-specific lenses

You can use regular SLR lenses with your dSLR camera, but you're not restricted to them.

There are choices in the form factor for some cameras, notably Nikon and Canon, when it comes to what type of lens to select. In the Nikon line, these are the DX series, and in Canons, it's EF-S lenses. Both of these lenses are designed specifically for digital cameras that use smaller image sensors. The advantage is the smaller size—they don't need to cover as large an image area for a smaller sensor and consequently can themselves be smaller and lighter. The second advantage is design. These lenses have been built specifically for digital sensors and do a very good job of directing the light in a way that works best with the sensor.

The drawbacks are selection and compatibility. Most digital-specific lenses are zooms, and there isn't anywhere near the range of focal lengths as with the standard lenses. And if you ever plan on moving to a camera with a 24mm x 36mm full-frame sensor (with a sensor as large as a 35mm frame of film), such as the Canon 1 DS Mark II, or if you choose to use a film camera on occasion, you won't be able to use these lenses.

Figure 3.4 *This image to the right was captured with a telephoto zoom lens. Because the boat was moving so fast, being able to change focal lengths allowed me to compose the image quickly. Photo taken with a Canon 1D Mk II, 70-200 with 2x converter at 1/640 and f/8.*

that doesn't change when the focal length is increased, such as the Canon 24-70 f/2.8 shown in **Figure 3.4**, is larger, heavier, and more expensive than a comparable lens with variable aperture. However, it does have an advantage in speed and in depth of field control. At the longer focal lengths you still have the wider, faster aperture setting giving you faster shutter speeds, and the narrower depth of field is often an advantage with composition (more on this in a bit).

Zoom lenses are great when you can't move closer to your subject, such as when shooting wildlife or distant objects. As an example, the hydroplane image in **Figure 3.5** would be very difficult to capture with a fixed-length lens. I was standing on the edge of the water and the boat was moving at well over 100 miles per hour, which required flexibility in framing that only a zoom lens would provide.

Figure 3.5 *Changing the focal length while capturing the image lets you create some interesting effects. Photo taken with a Canon 1Ds Mk II, 24-70 at 1/2 second and f/22.*

Wide-Angle Lenses

Wide-angle lenses (**Figure 3.6**) are a favorite of both landscape and indoor photographers because of their ability to capture large areas

Figure 3.6 *Wide-angle lenses, such as this 15-30mm zoom lens, are favorites with landscape and indoor photographers because of their ability to capture large areas in a frame.*

in a single image. *Wide-angle* is generally considered to be anything less than the 50mm focal length equivalent on 35mm film.

Wide-angle lenses in the 24-35mm focal length range are the most popular, letting you capture more in the frame without the distortion problems sometimes seen in wider lenses. True landscape fans will tell you that you can never get too wide, though, so 14-20mm is a popular choice with the outdoor crowd. To give you a practical example, the images shown in Figures 3.7 through 3.10 were all shot from exactly the same location with the same aperture. **Figure 3.7** was shot with a 50mm focal length and represents what is considered the normal focal length. **Figure 3.8** was captured at 35mm and still shows normal perspective, but with more of the house in the frame. In **Figure 3.9**, we've gone down to 24mm, and you can start to see the effects of wider angles where there is more of the foreground included in the scene, and the house is smaller. In the last example, **Figure 3.10**, you see the effect of photographing the scene with a 15mm lens. There is much more foreground included and the house has receded into the background. Remember, these were all photographed from exactly the same location.

Figure 3.7 *Here's the field of view with a 50mm, or standard-length lens. This most closely matches the human eye when looking at a scene.*

Figure 3.8 *At 35mm, there is more in the frame, but the perspective still looks close to normal with very little change in scale.*

Figure 3.9 *Moving to 24mm, there is much more area included in the image, with the main subject taking less prominence in the scene.*

Figure 3.10 *At 15mm, the ultra-wide-angle, includes all of the yard, making the house look further away than the other images.*

Although you can use a wide-angle lens as a conventional lens that just takes in more of a scene, these lenses really shine when used to their full potential in landscape. The greater depth of field with shorter focal lengths allows you to have more of your scene in sharp focus, as you can see in **Figures 3.11a** and **b**. Both of these images were taken with the same aperture, but in 3.11a you see less of the scene in focus when shot at 105mm compared to 3.11b, which was captured at 35mm. I kept the scene the same by cropping the 35mm image to show the same field of view.

Figure 3.11a *This image was captured at 105mm with a aperture of f/5.6; compare the areas in focus with the photo in Figure 3.11b.*

Figure 3.11b *With a 35mm lens, the same aperture of f/5.6 gives a greater depth of field which is easy to compare against Figure 3.11a.*

An effective way to use wide-angle lenses in your composition is to shoot low, with a foreground subject to draw the eye into the photo. As an example, compare **Figure 3.12**, shot at a normal standing height with no foreground object, to the image in **Figure 3.13** which was taken at the same location but at a lower position relative to the ground to emphasize the foreground object and lead your eye into the scene.

Figure 3.12 *Shooting landscapes with a wide-angle can give you a photo where everything appears small and loses impact. This shot was taken standing up with nothing to really give a visual clue as to distances.*

Figure 3.13 *By shooting from a lower position and including foreground detail, the scene now has more visual interest and scale.*

You'll also find wide-angle lenses useful when shooting indoors, capturing more of the room in your shot (**Figure 3.14**), and when shooting groups of people (**Figure 3.15**).

Figure 3.14 *Wide-angle lets you photograph more of an interior when shooting indoors.*

Figure 3.15 *Wide-angle lenses aren't just for landscapes and interiors. They are also useful when photographing groups of people.*

Finally, there is the ultra-wide-angle lens known as a *fisheye* lens, which comes in two flavors: the familiar *circular* frame, and the *full-frame* rectangular fisheye shown in **Figure 3.16**. Both types of fisheye lenses have extreme distortion, but that's part of the appeal to this type of image, and with proper composition fisheye lenses can make for very interesting effects.

Because a fisheye often has a 180-degree field of view, you really need to keep your eyes open for things like feet and arms that end up in the image (**Figure 3.17**).

Figure 3.16 *A full-frame fisheye lens gives you a normal-looking photograph with no dark corners.*

Figure 3.17 *Fisheye lenses capture a full 180-degree view of the world in front of you, usually with extreme distortion to straight lines. Watch for stray objects, like the arm on the left, when using one of these lenses!*

Standard Lenses

In the old film days it was common to have a camera come with a 50mm lens. This focal length gives you nearly the same field of view as the human eye.

Because a fixed focal-length lens isn't commonly included with a camera these days, a 50mm is often an early purchase choice for many photographers. These lenses are normally inexpensive, small, lightweight, and have a fast aperture (f/1.8 is not unusual, and if you're willing to spend more you can go as fast as f/1.2), making them ideal for shooting in low-light situations.

The standard range goes up to 90mm, which is a popular length for portrait work due to the flattering way it portrays the subject's face without distortion (**Figure 3.18**) and the unobtrusive working distance it allows between camera and subject.

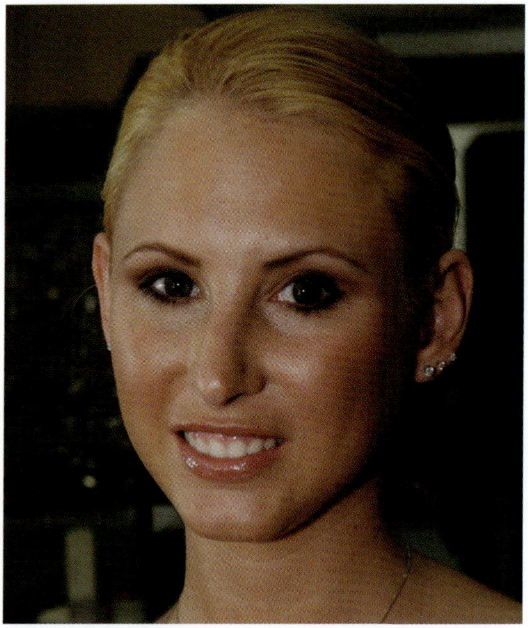

Figure 3.18 *A standard lens is typically in the 50mm to 90mm range. It gives you an angle of view that closely matches the human eye and perspective.*

Telephoto Lenses

For some reason, almost everyone starting out in photography wants a big telephoto lens. Are we compensating for some inadequacy? Probably not, but they look darn impressive and lend a professional look to the photographer carrying one around in the field (**Figure 3.19**).

Figure 3.19 *A telephoto lens, like this Canon 500mm, is ideal for capturing wildlife, but it's also useful in other types of photography.*

Telephoto lenses are any lenses with focal length over 90mm, going as high as 1000mm, although the most common sizes are 300mm and under, with a lens in the 200mm range being the most popular.

Where a wide-angle lens exaggerates the foreground and gives you a wide focus range, telephoto lenses compress objects and make them look closer together (**Figure 3.20**).

Figure 3.20 *Using a telephoto lens allows you to compress distant subjects, making them look closer together, like these trees which were actually a good distance apart from each other.*

A telephoto lens also has less depth of field at the same aperture than a shorter lens does, making focusing more critical and difficult. But, when you need the reach for a bird or animal that you can't or don't want to approach, nothing beats a big telephoto lens.

Most telephoto lenses are slower, with apertures of f/5.6 common in consumer-level lenses to keep the price and size down, meaning they are not great for low-light photography. As an example of the difference, consider two different Canon 400mm lenses. The EF 400 f/5.6 L is a fantastic lens that uses Canon's top optical glass and construction. This lens sells for about $1,100. The lens is 10 inches long and weighs about 2.8 pounds. The EF 400 f/2.8 gives you two more stops of aperture, or four times the light-gathering ability, but increases the size to 14 inches and 6.4 pounds. Oh, and the price? It jumps a bit as well, to $6,600.

Specialty Lenses

There is a whole world of lenses that don't quite fit into what would be considered "normal," although some of them can be used for normal purposes. The most popular of these types of lenses is the *macro* lens. Available in 60mm, 90-105mm, and 180mm focal lengths, macro lenses are optimized for focusing close-up and can reproduce subjects at life size, or at a 1:1 ratio, to show fine detail, or for photographing small objects (**Figure 3.21**).

Figure 3.21 *Macro lenses are popular choices for photographing details and small subjects. They allow you to capture images up to life size, or 1:1. They can also be used for other purposes, making them a good all-around lens.*

The longer macro lenses are often used as portrait lenses but you need to be careful—this is one case where your optics can actually be too sharp!

Going a step further, Canon has a special macro lens for extreme close-ups, the MP-E 65mm (**Figure 3.22**). This lens is able to reproduce everything from life size 1:1 up to five times life size, 5:1. You can forget auto-focus with this lens, and depth of field, especially at high magnifications, is minimal (**Figure 3.23**).

Figure 3.22 *The Canon MP-E 65 is a unique macro lens. You can photograph anything from life size to 5x life size. Because there is no focus control on the lens, all focusing is done by moving the camera.*

Figure 3.23 *The MP-E 65 lets you get up to 5x the actual size of your subject, but the depth of field is very shallow, making this a challenging lens to use successfully.*

Another fun lens, and one that's affordable to almost anyone, is the Lensbaby (www.lensbaby.com) shown in **Figure 3.24**. This unique lens has a flexible body that lets you set the area of sharp focus where you want and throw the rest of the image into soft focus. By simply moving the lens in or out, and angling it (**Figure 3.25**), you can create some amazing effects that would be impossible otherwise without spending hours in Photoshop.

Figure 3.24 *The Lensbaby is available for different camera systems, and it's one of the most unusual and fun tools you can carry around.*

Figure 3.25 *By moving the Lensbaby in or out and bending it, you can control which areas of your image are in focus and which are soft. It's a fun way to experiment with new looks.*

The image shown in **Figure 3.26** was used as my holiday card last year. The Lensbaby let me capture the center of the poinsettia in sharp focus while throwing the edges into soft focus, giving me an interesting effect that lets my image stand out from the typical shot.

Tip

Don't go wild with lenses when you're just starting out. By learning to use one or two lenses well, you'll have a better understanding of what you want and need in a lens before shelling out a lot of money that you might not need to spend at all. I suggest getting two zoom lenses that cover the 24mm to 300mm range and learning your system inside out before moving on to other lenses.

Figure 3.26 *I used a Lensbaby to get the soft focus look around this poinsettia for my holiday card last year.*

Other specialty lenses include *teleconverters* (**Figure 3.27**), which magnify any lens they are used with by either 1.4x or 2x. These converters have a drawback, though. A 1.4x converter will cost you one f-stop, turning an f/5.6 300mm lens into an f/8 420mm lens. Be sure that your camera can still auto-focus with the slower aperture. When you use a 2x converter on the same lens, you lose two stops, ending up with an f/11 600mm lens that almost certainly won't auto-focus.

Figure 3.27 *Teleconverters, like these from Canon, extend the reach of your lenses. Canon has 1.4x and 2.0x converters available for auto focus lenses.*

4 Digital Photography Techniques

Shooting with a digital SLR isn't all that different from using any other camera, film or digital. If you're coming from the film world, you'll appreciate the immediate feedback you get from the LCD screen and the flexibility of changing ISO settings as needed for changing light conditions.

If you're coming from a compact digital camera (which I've been calling a *digicam*), you have an adjustment to make if you are used to using the LCD to compose your photos before capturing them—with one exception, dSLR cameras don't have a live preview on the LCD. Instead, you look through the camera's lens for a *live* preview.

In this chapter, I cover the common features you'll find in a dSLR, including metering, exposure adjustments, and composition.

Selecting the Metering Mode

Before getting into the different metering modes, it's helpful to understand how a camera light meter works. When you press the shutter button part way, the camera activates an internal light meter, which reads the light values coming into the camera to determine what the proper exposure is. It works this bit of magic by considering the subject as middle gray. How much of the subject is included in this measurement is determined by the *mode* you select. All dSLRs have some form of evaluative metering and center-weighted metering, and some dSLRs also include a spot-metering mode. Let's take a closer look at each of these and when you'd select one over the other.

Evaluative metering

Evaluative metering (Canon and Sigma) is called *matrix* metering in the Nikon world, *honeycomb* by Sony, *ESP* by Olympus, and *segment* by Pentax. By whatever name, evaluative metering works by dividing the image area into sections like those in **Figure 4.1**.

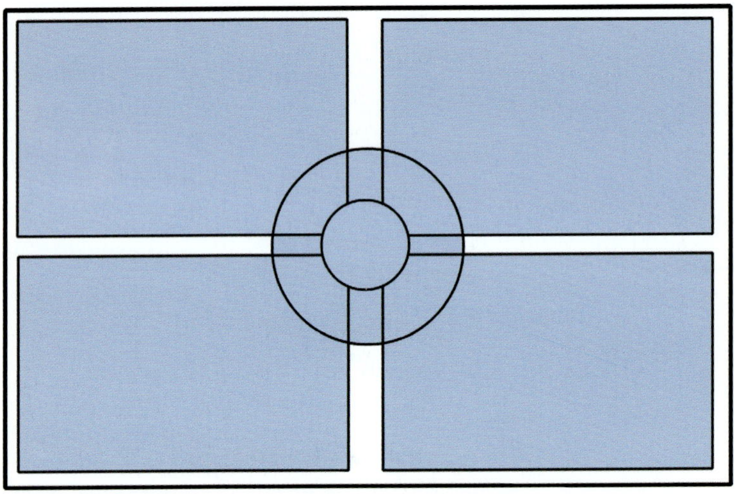

Figure 4.1 *Camera meters work by dividing the viewfinder into segments that are evaluated for lighting values. The number of segments varies by camera model.*

The number of segments varies widely from one camera to the next, with some using fewer measurements, like the Sigma which uses 14, up to the Nikon, which uses up to 1,005.

The meter reads the light value from each of these segments and averages them out to obtain the best overall exposure, which is the one that keeps the most information within the range the sensor is capable of recording, from dark to light. This is one area in which dSLR cameras really excel over their compact cousins. Because the dSLR sensor is much larger, it's able to record a wider range of light values (see Chapter 1 for a complete run-down on how the sensor records light).

Center-weighted metering

Center-weighted metering concentrates the measurement of light on the central area of the image area. This allows you to get a more accurate reading for a critical portion of the scene and works well when there is a fairly even range of light values in the scene. **Figure 4.2** shows an example of the area measured by center-weighted metering.

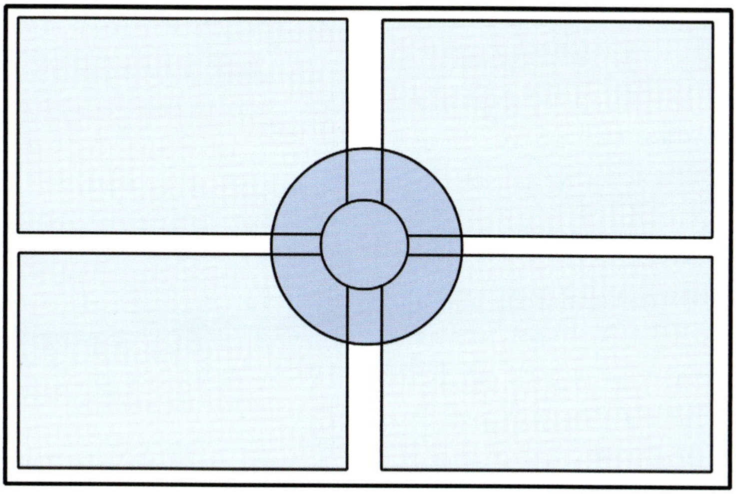

Figure 4.2 *In center-weighted metering modes, the camera uses the central part of the viewfinder to make the exposure decision.*

A derivative of center-weighted metering is *center-weighted evaluative* metering, where the entire image area is considered when determining exposure, but more emphasis is placed on the central area of the image.

Spot metering

Spot metering, typically available on mid-level and pro-level cameras, measures only a specific area of the image, often as little as 3 percent of the total scene, to determine exposure. On some cameras, the spot meter is fixed on the center of the viewfinder; on others, such as the Canon, you can set the meter to read from any of the auto-focus points. **Figures 4.3** and **4.4** show examples of spot-metering modes.

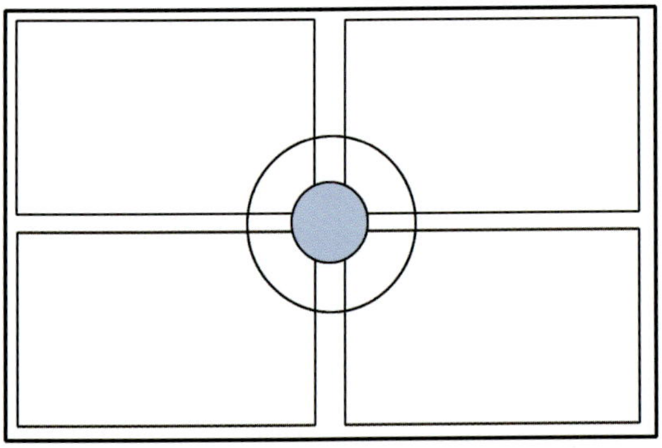

Figure 4.3 *Many cameras also have a spot-metering mode that uses a very small area of the viewfinder to base the exposure on. This mode is best when working in difficult lighting situations.*

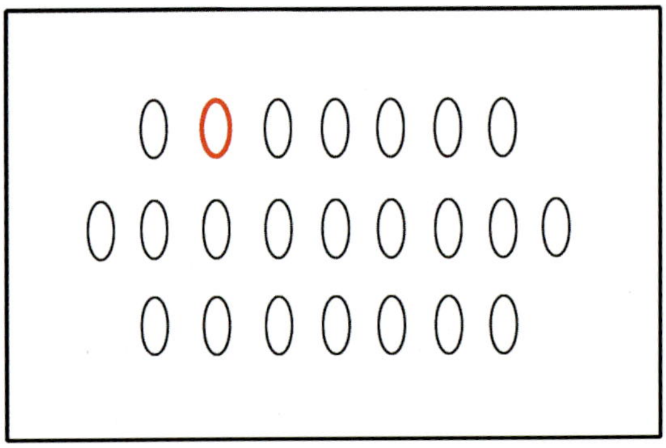

Figure 4.4 *More advanced cameras, such as the Canon 1Ds Mark II, can use any of the auto-focus points as the location for metering. The selected spot is shown in red.*

Spot metering is the best choice when you have a specific area of the image that is critical for exposure. An example of this would be photographing a person against a very bright or very dark background, a situation which causes evaluative metering to over- or underexpose the main subject. If your camera doesn't include a spot-metering mode, you would choose center-weighted in such an example.

Choosing the Proper Exposure

With all these choices, how do you decide which is best? The evaluative modes are normally the best choice for the typical shooting situation. As good as evaluative metering is, though, there are times when you need to override the camera's suggested exposure to get the best results. In this section, I take a look at how to handle these situations to get the proper exposure and avoid those disappointments from exposure problems.

How exposure is determined

As I said earlier in this chapter, the exposure meter in your camera works by reading the light that is being reflected back to the sensor. It uses this information to find the range of tones from dark to light. When you use evaluative metering, the camera determines what the middle point in that range should be. As an example, take a look at the image in **Figure 4.5**.

Figure 4.5 *This image has a total range of ten stops of light, which is near the upper end of what a dSLR sensor can capture.*

The range of light is measured as *exposure value* (EV), with low numbers being darker than higher numbers. When the scene is measured, the darkest area has a reading of EV2, while the lightest

> **Note**
>
> You can increase the amount of detail captured by shooting in the raw format. Chapter 7 has full details on raw capture and how it can work for you.

is assigned EV12, a total range of ten stops of light. In this example, the camera would likely choose an exposure setting that would be equal to EV7, which is the middle of the range.

If the sensor in your camera is able to handle ten stops of light values, everything is fine, and you'll have detail throughout the image from dark to light. But what if you can't capture the full range of light in your scene?

In that case, you want to expose for the critical details in your image. If that means bringing out detail in dark clothing, or shadows, you'll want to expose for that at the expense of highlight detail. If clouds, snow, or whites are the critical element in your image, you need to expose for that and let the shadows lose detail if needed.

Digital cameras are more sensitive to highlights than to shadows, so the normal method of exposure is to meter for the brightest part of the subject you want detail in. You'll be able to recover shadow detail much easier than highlights with Photoshop CS2 or Photoshop Elements.

Using exposure compensation

All dSLRs allow you to make adjustments to the suggested exposure through an *exposure compensation* feature. Depending on your camera, this might be in 1/2- or 1/3-stop increments. Compensation works by changing the suggested exposure to allow more or less light for a specific situation. As an example, the image shown in **Figure 4.6** was shot with the suggested meter reading.

> **Tip**
>
> Whenever you're shooting in a mixed or difficult lighting situation, I suggest capturing a test image to review before shooting a series of images. This way you can make adjustments immediately, potentially saving a shoot that might otherwise be ruined.

The highlights are lighter than I wanted, so I recaptured the shot with a -2/3 (that's a negative 2/3) compensation setting. This reduced the amount of light during the exposure, similar to changing the aperture or shutter speed but in a finer increment than either of those choices would have given me. After a -2/3 adjustment, I ended up with the image shown in **Figure 4.7**, which has more highlight detail and is closer to the photo I had in my mind.

Figure 4.6 Sometimes the suggested exposure isn't the best choice. Here the highlights are overexposed.

Figure 4.7 By using exposure compensation, I've reduced the exposure by 2/3 of a stop, giving me more detail.

How can you tell when exposure compensation is the right choice? After all, if you wait until you get home or back to the computer to review your images, the odds are against being able to go back and capture the same image again. This is where digital rules the roost—the LCD display with histogram gives you immediate feedback on your images.

In **Figure 4.8**, you can see the histogram from the overexposed example shown in **Figure 4.6**. The detail in the highlights is pushed against the right side of the histogram, indicating overexposure.

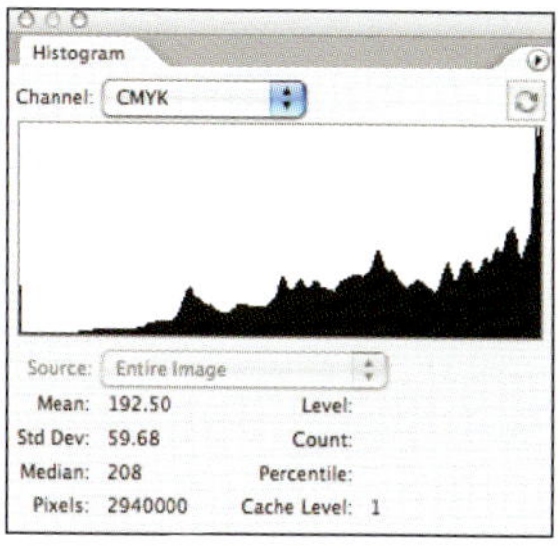

Figure 4.8 Here's the original histogram with the suggested exposure. You can see that the highlights are pushing against the right side of the histogram, indicating lost detail.

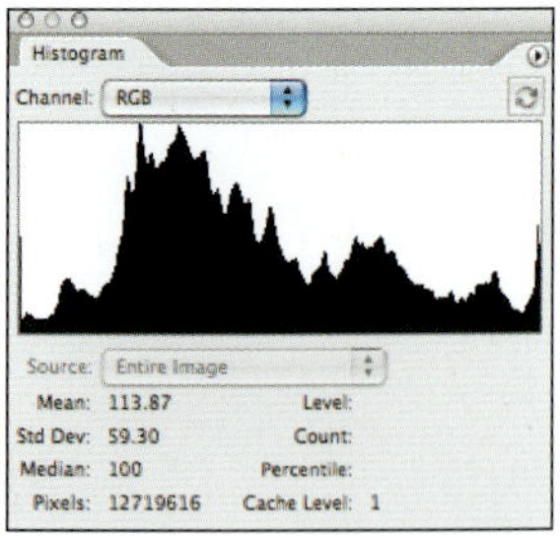

Figure 4.9 *After the exposure compensation, all the data is within the range of the histogram.*

After the -2/3-stop compensation, the histogram has moved to the left, giving me more detail in the highlights, which I was trying to capture (**Figure 4.9**).

If you're faced with rapidly changing light situations, you can also use *exposure bracketing.* On most cameras, exposure bracketing captures a set of three images: one with a minus exposure, one at the suggested exposure, and the final image with more than the suggested exposure. You can often set the amount of compensation, but I typically use a 1/2-stop increment in both directions to ensure that one of the images is accurately exposed. For specifics on exposure bracketing for your camera, refer to your manual. **Figures 4.10a** through **4.10c** show what a typical bracketed exposure does.

Figure 4.10a *With exposure bracketing you capture three or more images. This is the first exposure, which is 1/2 stop below the recommended setting.*

Figure 4.10b *The second exposure in the bracketed set is at the suggested exposure.*

Figure 4.10c *The third and final exposure is 1/2 stop over the recommended setting.*

Handling dark subjects

Because the light meter in your camera is set to record whatever it measures as a medium tone (18% gray to be exact), dark subjects sometimes become overexposed in an effort to lighten up the midtones. To compensate for this, you can either use exposure compensation or switch to spot metering, if your camera supports it, and meter off a lighter-colored subject.

Most cameras have the ability to lock exposure information and let you recompose before capturing the photo. This is often done in Single Shot Focus mode by simply focusing on a subject and keeping the shutter pressed halfway while you recompose. Alternatively, if your camera has an exposure lock button, you can use this to get a meter reading. The selected metering will be kept until the photo is taken, letting you change focal length, focus, or composition. Once the shutter is pressed, and the image captured, the exposure lock is released, and you're ready to shoot the next image.

For images with large amounts of very dark areas, exposure compensation of as much as two f-stops may be needed. For example, in **Figure 4.11** I shot this scene at the metered settings.

Figure 4.11 *Dark images can be overexposed by the typical meter, like this example shows.*

As you can see, the black areas are more of a gray tone due to the meter trying to make this area a midtone. In **Figure 4.12**, I used a -1 2/3 stop exposure compensation to keep the rich blacks in the original subject.

Figure 4.12 *To return the blacks back to where they should be, I used a -1 2/3-stop exposure compensation.*

Handling light subjects

Unless you're a fan of gray snow, or off-color whites in general, shooting bright objects requires exposure adjustment as well. Like the exposure for dark subjects, when the camera meter evaluates a light scene, such as a snowy landscape, it tries to render the scene with the snow as a midtone, causing it to come out gray or bluish.

In **Figure 4.13**, I shot at the recommended exposure. As you can see, the whites are not very bright at all.

Figure 4.13 *Bright scenes have the same problem as dark ones. The meter attempts to make the main subject a middle tone, giving gray colors rather than good whites.*

By using exposure compensation and capturing the image with an additional +2 stops, the snow is back to a clean white while still retaining detail.

Figure 4.14 *By adding +2 exposure compensation, the whites are where they should be.*

Backlighting

Backlit scenes are the most difficult ones for a camera meter to handle properly. You typically have a very bright light source, such as the sun, overwhelming the meter with light. To compensate, the camera meter attempts to bring the brightest light into range, which means you often have only a silhouette of the person or other subject.

In cases like this, using center-weighted or spot metering is the best option, since you'll usually be able to meter off just the subject and exclude the bright background. For example, **Figure 4.15** shows a photo captured at the camera's evaluative reading.

By switching to spot metering, I'm able to change what the main source of light is and come up with the image shown in **Figure 4.16**. This is a change of three full stops from the original reading, and although I've lost detail in the brightest areas of the image, I can now see what the subject is.

Tip

The best solution with backlighting is to use a flash to help fill in the light. You'll find more on flash photography in Chapter 5.

Figure 4.15 *In the typical backlight situation, the camera meter is overwhelmed by the background light, making the main subject underexposed.*

Figure 4.16 *By switching to spot metering, I can get a better exposure setting, giving me details in the subject at the expense of the background.*

When you can't switch to a different metering mode for some reason, it's time to get creative by using the alternate techniques covered earlier in this chapter. The best way to deal with this, if possible, is to meter the sky without the sun in the frame (assuming you are shooting towards the sun) or meter the ground or a bush. A final alternative is to move in close to your subject so that it fills the frame and then take a meter reading. If your camera has an exposure lock button, set the exposure and then move into your shooting position to compose and capture the photo.

Creative Techniques

Your new dSLR most likely came with various shooting modes designed to make it easy for you to shoot different subjects with optimal settings. But the optimal settings don't always translate into the most compelling images. In this section, I take a look at some of the various modes and explain why you might want to override those settings. In the process, you learn more about exposure options, allowing you to move away from the shooting modes when you're ready to take your photography to a new level of control.

Portraits

By default, Portrait mode gives you a minimum depth of field to blur out backgrounds like the one shown in **Figure 4.17**. Depending on the type of portrait you want to capture, a blurred background might be just the opposite of what you want.

It's getting more and more popular to take environmental portraits, where the subject is in a familiar setting that shows them in their element. In this example, you'd want more depth of field in order to show that environment with the subject. For this type of portrait, you need to switch to Aperture Priority. In **Figure 4.18** you can see the result of shooting in Aperture Priority with a setting of f/8 on a telephoto lens.

The subject and immediate surroundings are in sharp focus, and the distant background is still blurred, giving you the best of both worlds.

Figure 4.17 *The typical image captured in Portrait mode has a minimal depth of field, which is often the correct setting.*

Figure 4.18 *When you want to include some of the surroundings in the image, switching from Portrait mode to Aperture Priority is the way to go.*

Landscapes

This mode is the opposite of Portrait mode, giving you the maximum possible depth of field while still keeping the shutter speed high enough to handhold the camera. In low-light situations, which are usually the best for landscape, such as sunrise and sunset, this means less depth of field than you want for a landscape image. Once again, it's Aperture Priority to the rescue.

As an example, the image shown in **Figure 4.19** would have been nearly impossible to capture using Landscape mode, so I used Aperture Priority along with a tripod for a 1/4-second exposure.

Note

You'll have better results using a tripod whenever possible. There's a common rule in photography that says you shouldn't try to handhold your camera for any exposure longer than the focal length of your lens (roughly). In other words, if you're using a 50mm lens, you shouldn't handhold anything slower than 1/60 second.

Figure 4.19 *In low-light situations, Landscape mode may not work for you. In this case, I used Aperture Priority along with a tripod to get a longer exposure.*

Night photography

One of the advantages of a dSLR is that you can take longer exposures than you can with a digicam. Although many dSLRs include a Night mode, it's often not a very long exposure (although it is long enough that you'll need a tripod), seldom more than one second. By switching to Manual mode, you can use the *bulb* setting. Bulb is a holdover term from the old days when a shutter release was triggered by using a blast of air through a handheld bulb. Today, bulb means the shutter stays open as long as the shutter button is pressed. Most cameras have an optional cable release or remote shutter release that can be used for this purpose, letting you take photos that can be as long as your batteries last. As an example, **Figure 4.20** shows a 16-minute exposure used to capture star trails. By pointing the camera at the north star and leaving the shutter open for long periods of time, you can capture the movement of the stars across the sky.

Figure 4.20 *Star trails take longer to capture than Night mode can deal with. In this case, it's time to switch to Manual mode and use a cable release for a one hour or more exposure.*

For more down-to-earth night photography, capturing images of fireworks is a popular subject, and once again bulb mode is the proper choice. For the examples shown in **Figures 4.21** and **4.22**, I used exposures of 6 seconds and 8 seconds at f/22 to record multiple bursts of fireworks along with their trails.

Figure 4.21 *A six-second exposure lets me capture multiple bursts of fireworks.*

Figure 4.22 *Don't be afraid to experiment. Here I've used a eight-second exposure to photograph more bursts with longer trails.*

Macro and close-up photography

In macro or close-up photography, you normally want the most depth of field possible. Because the working distances are so short, even an aperture of f/16 doesn't give you much depth of field. But, as with the other examples, you don't always want the typical setting. There are times when a more artistic look is desired. For example, **Figure 4.23** shows what type of image macro mode can give you at a small aperture of f/16.

Figure 4.23 *This is a typical macro mode photo, with maximum depth of field.*

In the next example, **Figure 4.24**, I've used a wider aperture to reduce the depth of field. By changing to f/8, only the ends of the stamen are in focus, giving me a nice soft background.

Figure 4.24 *By moving to Aperture Priority, I reduced the depth of field to give me a more artistic look.*

Sports photography

After all the previous examples, you may be wondering why your camera even has a Shutter Priority mode. When you shoot in Shutter Priority mode (sometimes called Sports mode), you're optimizing the exposure for a fast shutter speed to let you freeze action, as **Figure 4.25** shows.

But static images where all action is stopped isn't always the best choice for showing action. By switching to Shutter Priority and choosing a slower shutter speed, you can capture the motion in the scene, giving your photo a feeling of life and activity like the one shown in **Figure 4.26**.

PHOTO BY LAURENCE CHEN

Figure 4.25 *Sports mode optimizes the shutter speed to freeze action.*

Figure 4.26 *Switching to Shutter Priority and slowing the exposure down lets you capture motion in your sports shots.*

5 Flash Photography

When the lights go down, you have two choices if you want to keep shooting: either increase the ISO setting or start using a flash. You don't have to wait until it's dark for flash to be useful, though. Flash can be a great addition in any kind of light when you need to fill in shadows or add a twinkle to someone's eyes.

Built-in Flash

Almost all of the entry-level and mid-level digital SLR cameras come with a built-in flash that pops up when needed (**Figure 5.1**). For many people, this is all the flash they'll ever need. It's always there, never needs additional batteries, and doesn't take up extra space in the bag or pocket. However, a built-in flash is not always a panacea.

***Figure 5.1** All entry-level and most mid-level dSLRs come with a built-in flash. It's handy to have and always ready, but doesn't give you the flexibility of an external flash.*

Built-in gotchas

The drawbacks to a built-in flash are flexibility and power—basically, you don't get either with these flashes. Because the flash folds into the camera body, it's small and can't be adjusted to different angles (more on this later). You can see the size difference between a built-in flash and an external flash in **Figure 5.2**. This relates closely to the second issue: power.

Figure 5.2 *Comparing the size of the flash tube to a external flash, it's easy to see why you don't have the range or power you get with the external unit.*

Flash strength is measured by *guide number*, or GN. To determine how close your subject must be to be lit up by the flash, divide the GN number by the aperture, and the resulting number gives you the effective distance of your flash in meters. So if you read a flash strength of GN=13 at ISO 100, that means if you want to shoot at f/4, the flash will reach about 3.3 meters, or 10 feet.

Another issue with the built-in flash is related to drawback number one above. Because the flash is so close to the lens, red-eye is a common problem when using these flashes with people or animals. Most cameras have a red-eye reduction mode to ease this effect, though, so let's take a look at that.

Tech Note: Flash and the Inverse Square Law

If you're interested in how the light from your flash really works, it follows something called the inverse square law, which says that a subject twice as far receives only a quarter of the light from the same source. In other words, something that is 5 feet away from the flash is going to have four times as much light hitting it as the same object when it's 10 feet away. This is why backgrounds go dark so quickly when using flash as the main light source.

Red-eye reduction

When the light source is too close to the lens, red-eye becomes an issue. It's such a common problem that almost every camera out today has a red-eye reduction mode. This works by firing one or more pre-flashes to prevent the actual flash from capturing the reflection in your subject's eyes (**Figure 5.3**).

PHOTO BY LAURENCE CHEN

Figure 5.3 *Red-eye is a common problem with flash photography, especially when using a built-in flash unit.*

It doesn't always eliminate the problem, but typically using red-eye reduction mode will lessen the amount of time you need to spend in your image editor fixing up your friend's eyes so they don't look bloodshot.

Red-eye reduction causes a slight delay in the capture of your image. When you press the shutter release, the flash needs to send these pre-flashes out before the actual image is captured, which can lead to shots with people in a different position than planned.

External Flash

When you find yourself wishing you could light up subjects from farther away or light larger groups of people, an external flash is the way to go. Where the built-in flash that you might have with your camera is limited in strength to a GN of 15 or so, an external flash like the Canon 580EX has a GN of 58 at ISO 100. For that same shot at f/4 that we were able to get 10 feet of lighting from with the built-in flash, we are now getting 48 feet.

Bounce flash

Direct flash can be very harsh and not at all flattering to your subject. In fact, the term "deer in the headlights" comes to mind in many cases when photographing people with direct flash mounted on the camera. Most external flash units can be swiveled and tilted, as shown in **Figure 5.4**, to bounce the light off a wall or ceiling,

Figure 5.4 *Setting the flash to bounce off a wall or ceiling can soften the light.*

giving a much softer look. By way of contrast, in **Figure 5.5** the subjects were photographed with an external flash mounted on the camera and aimed straight at the subjects.

Figure 5.5 *Here's an example of shooting with the flash pointed right at the subjects. The light is strong and harsh, with heavy shadows.*

As you can see, there are harsh highlights and dark shadows from the intense light coming straight at them. By adjusting the flash head up and bouncing the light off the ceiling, the lighting is much more indirect and softer, with less of a strong shadow (**Figure 5.6**).

Figure 5.6 *Bouncing the flash off the ceiling spreads the light and gives a much more pleasant look.*

If you don't have a ceiling handy, or your ceiling isn't a neutral color, you can bounce the flash off a card that either comes with the flash unit or is taped onto the flash, as shown in **Figure 5.7**.

The same techniques can be used to bounce light off a wall by swiveling the head to the side as shown in **Figure 5.8**, which is a useful method when shooting outdoors with your subject near a wall to help fill in shadows.

Figure 5.7 *Most external flash units come with a built-in bounce card that can be used outdoors.*

Figure 5.8 *Using the swivel feature on an external flash works similarly to tilting to bounce off a ceiling, but it's an effective way to bounce light when all you have is a wall.*

Remote flash

Many of the top-end flash units from companies like Canon and Nikon include support for using the flash as a *slave*, meaning that it only fires when it sees another flash go off. These flashes often work wirelessly, letting you set up multiple flashes to get the best possible lighting conditions (**Figure 5.9**). Essentially, you're turning your flash units into studio type lights.

PHOTO BY LAURENCE CHEN

Figure 5.9 *Many flash units can work as slaves, being triggered when they see the light from another flash.*

Sync modes

Flash has different sync modes, or ways of synchronizing with the shutter when you capture an image. Every camera has a maximum sync speed which is the fastest shutter speed you can use and still get a full image. If you go beyond this shutter speed, you'll end up with a black band through your photo like the one shown in **Figure 5.10**.

Figure 5.10 *If your shutter speed is too fast for the flash, you'll have a photo that is partially black like the lower half of this shot.*

In general, a sync speed of 1/125 is commonly the high end for entry- and mid-level digital cameras. In other words, the fastest shutter speed you can use is 1/125, and you'll need to adjust your aperture to stay within this maximum.

The duration of the flash is much shorter than the actual exposure though, often as little as 1/15,000 of a second. Because of this, it's possible to see motion in your photos along with sharp frozen detail. To give you control over this, there are sync modes that you can select to tell the camera when to fire the flash.

- **Front sync**, or *front curtain*, fires the flash at the start of the exposure. With a moving subject, you can get some odd effects because the blur and motion will appear in front of the sharp image as shown in **Figure 5.11**.

PHOTO BY LAURENCE CHEN

Figure 5.11 *Using front curtain sync freezes the action at the start of the exposure, with any movement recorded in front f the flash.*

- **Rear sync**, or *rear curtain*, fires the flash at the end of the exposure, making it ideal for use with moving subjects (**Figure 5.12**).

PHOTO BY LAURENCE CHEN

Figure 5.12 *Rear curtain sync is best when you have motion and want the movement to trail the sharp details.*

- **Slow sync** allows you to use a slower than normal shutter speed to include background detail (**Figure 5.13**) which would otherwise be lost in a normal flash exposure.

Tip

Don't be afraid to experiment. Sometimes the motion can be a great addition to your image, giving it some life or mystery. Learn to master your flash, and you have a whole new world of photography to enjoy.

PHOTO BY LAURENCE CHEN

Figure 5.13 *Slow sync is used when you want to include natural light in the scene as well as flash.*

Obviously, unless you want to have movement in the image, you'll need to use a tripod and avoid subjects that move when using this mode of flash. But it can be a very effective way of recording more of the detail in a scene.

6 Filters and Special Effects

There are some looks and effects in photography that can still be best achieved by using special equipment on the camera. Read on to find out how to use filters and special effects to spice up your images.

Filters

It might surprise you to know that filters still have a very valuable place in the digital camera bag. Sure, you can simulate many of the effects of a filter in Photoshop after the fact, but not everything lends itself to software adjustments. In some cases, you'll have better results from the beginning by using the appropriate tools with your camera when you go out to photograph.

UV filters

I'll be very up front on this one. I am not a fan of UV (ultraviolet) filters. Most of them are sold with a lens by a salesperson in a camera store looking for a quick profit. This usually goes along with, "Do you want a UV filter to protect that lens?"—the theory being that when you drop your expensive new lens or something pokes it, the filter will prevent the glass element of the lens from being damaged. This is probably true—it will likely prevent damage to the glass, but so will using the lens hood, which does do an even better job (trust me on this one—I've had enough practice to know that a lens hood *does* protect a lens when you drop it).

But the biggest issue I have with the typical UV filter that is pushed on the unsuspecting buyer is quality. You've just spent a good amount of money to buy the best lens you could afford, and now the salesperson wants you to slap a cheap piece of glass in front of it? Does that really make sense?

Tip

If you're going to use a UV filter, I recommend getting a top-quality one from a company such as B+W, Nikon, Canon, or Tiffen.

UV filters do help to reduce the ultraviolet light (hence the UV name) reaching your sensor, which is helpful when shooting at high elevations. So, it's more effective if you're shooting in the mountains than at a park in Los Angeles.

There is one instance where I highly recommend having something like a UV filter on your camera. If you're shooting in windy conditions where there is sand blowing, by all means put a filter over your lens. Sand will pit the coatings on a lens faster than you think, potentially ruining the optical quality.

Polarizers

There is one filter I never leave home without. My *polarizer* is by far the most used filter in my kit, and for good reason. A polarizing filter can make a world of difference to your images in many different situations. The first thing that comes to mind for most people is bluer skies, which is maximized when the sun is 90 degrees to the direction you're shooting (**Figure 6.1**), but that's really just the beginning of what these amazing filters can do for you.

Figure 6.1 *A polarizing filter is one of the most useful additions you can carry in your camera bag.*

Along with enhancing the color of skies, which also helps clouds stand out in more detail, a polarizer is perfect for dealing with reflections in water and glass. **Figure 6.2** shows a photo taken with no polarizer. Although you can see the fish through the glass, the image is ruined by the reflections.

In **Figure 6.3**, I used a polarizer to remove the reflection, giving me much cleaner view of the fish through the glass.

Figure 6.2 *With no polarizer filter, the glass causes problems with reflections.*

Figure 6.3 *By using a polarizer, I've removed the reflection and made the fish easier to see.*

The same works with water when you want to reduce or remove reflections on the surface. By rotating the ring of the filter, you can control how strong the polarizing effect is on the subject. In **Figure 6.4**, I used the polarizer to remove the reflections and allow me to capture what's under the surface of the water—something that would have been impossible without the filter.

Figure 6.4 *You can also use a polarizing filter to reduce reflections in water to see what's under the surface.*

One disadvantage of using a polarizer is that you lose light. The amount depends on how the filter is adjusted, but it's typically a loss of one to two f-stops. If you recall from Chapter 2, where I cover exposure, this means that if your shutter speed is 1/125 at f/16, with a filter you would then be shooting 1/60 or 1/30 at f/16 to compensate for the polarizer. This can work to your advantage, though, especially when you have bright lighting and want to use a slower exposure than you are able to get with normal metering. In cases like this, the polarizer can be used like a *neutral-density* filter (see later in this chapter) to give you a couple of extra stops of light—perfect for those time that you want to capture a waterfall with blurred motion.

Another great use for a polarizing filter that might not be obvious at first is in rainy conditions, particularly when photographing landscape details. The polarizer can pull color detail out in the image that would otherwise be lost (**Figure 6.5**).

In the example shown in **Figure 6.6**, I used a polarizer to increase the saturation of the leaves. Even though there was no direct sunlight, the filter worked its magic to bring life to the subject. Compare this image to Figure 6.5 to see what you think.

Figure 6.5 *In this image, shot on a overcast day with flat light, the subject doesn't really stand out from the surroundings.*

Figure 6.6 *With a polarizing filter, the color saturation is much better.*

You do need to be aware of how you are using your polarizer, though. Particularly for landscapes, it's easy to just set it for a maximum effect that often looks artificial (**Figure 6.7**).

Figure 6.7 *Be careful not to overuse the polarizing filter, though. You can end up with an image like this one that looks artificial.*

This is even more problematic at higher elevations where too strong of a setting can make the sky go nearly black. Figures 6.8 through 6.10 are a set of images showing different polarization settings. **Figure 6.8** uses no polarization, which leaves the sky washed out.

Going to the other extreme, **Figure 6.9** has set the filter to the maximum strength. Although there is certainly more detail in the clouds, and the sky is much bluer, it just doesn't look natural—at least not for this planet.

Adjusting the filter down from the maximum, I finally ended up with **Figure 6.10**, about a quarter turn back down from the maximum. This setting gave me what I felt was the most realistic version of the sky, with just a slight improvement in color and contrast over what my eye was able to see.

Tip

It's fine to enhance reality or even make your own, depending on what you're going for. But if you want realism, small enhancements are the best way to go.

Figure 6.8 *With no filter, the sky is washed out with little color or contrast.*

Figure 6.9 *This image is captured with the polarizing filter set to the maximum effect.*

Figure 6.10 *Here's the final image with about 1/4 of the maximum strength.*

Color enhancers

I don't consider a color enhancer a critical filter to have in your camera bag, but it's a nice addition that can make the difference between normal and exceptional. **Figure 6.11** shows a scene with no filter attached. It's nice, but nothing really special. Adding a color-enhancing filter boosts the colors, especially the reds, as shown in **Figure 6.12**.

Figure 6.11 *Color-enhancing filters can turn a subject like this one, which looks washed out, into one like Figure 6.12.*

Figure 6.12 *With a color-enhancing filter this image looks much better, especially in the red tones.*

You can accomplish much the same effect in Photoshop by adjusting saturation of the red channel. I will show you how to do that later in this chapter.

IR filters

IR, or infrared, filters are something you either love or hate. Personally, I'm in the love camp. I'm constantly fascinated at the results when shooting with an IR filter on my camera.

Shooting with an IR filter is totally alien, though. To begin with, an IR filter cuts out all visible light. Yep, you don't see a thing when you have an IR filter attached to your lens. So how do you shoot with one of these on your camera? You use manual focus and metering. Focus on your subject without the filter attached. Then attach the filter and set your exposure to about three seconds to start (yes, you will be using a tripod). The great part about shooting IR with digital is that you can see the results on the LCD and make needed adjustments to the exposure based on the histogram.

The image shown in **Figure 6.13** was taken in midday, but because of the filter it required a five-second exposure. There was a bit of a breeze blowing, so there is some movement in the leaves, but I think this adds to the appeal of the image.

Figure 6.13 *An IR filter adds a very different look to your images. This one required a very long exposure (about 5 seconds).*

Compare this to a similar image shot with no filter (**Figure 6.14**). As I said earlier, you either love IR or hate it. For me, seeing a hidden world is worth the effort. Foliage in IR is white, whereas nonliving things don't show any change in tone.

Figure 6.14 *This shot, taken within minutes of the one shown in Figure 6.13, shows what the scene looks like with no filter.*

You can also simulate IR in software with filters that work in Photoshop (I will show you how a bit later in this chapter). The effect isn't quite the same, but you can do pretty well with it.

Soft-focus filters

Now why would you ever want to use a filter that intentionally softens your photo? Soft focus has been a portrait photography favorite for years, especially for glamour style images (**Figure 6.15**). More recently, it's become popular with other photography styles as well. As an example, the exceptional landscape photographer Tony Sweet uses a Soft Ray filter from Singh-Ray (www.singh-ray.com/sweet.html)

that he helped design. To see what an amazing job this filter can do, take a look at **Figures 6.16a** and **16.b**.

Soft-focus filters are often used in portrait and glamour photography to add an ethereal and dreamy style to the image. It is quite flattering to portraits because it hides blemishes and softens the skin.

Figure 6.15 *Soft-focus lenses have been popular for decades, especially with portrait photographers.*

PHOTO BY TONY SWEET (WWW.TONYSWEET.COM)

Figure 6.16a *A new filter from Singh-Ray takes soft focus a step further. Here's the before image.*

PHOTO BY TONY SWEET (WWW.TONYSWEET.COM)

Figure 6.16b *And here's the after version with the Singh-Ray Soft Ray filter.*

By dissipating the light beyond normal limits and boundaries, the Soft-Ray imparts a soft, mystical mood over the landscape.

Neutral-density filters

Neutral-density filters are used to reduce the amount of light reaching the sensor. These filters come in both graduated and solid styles (**Figure 6.17**) and can make the difference between getting a shot that has harsh lighting and contrast or missing out on the opportunity altogether.

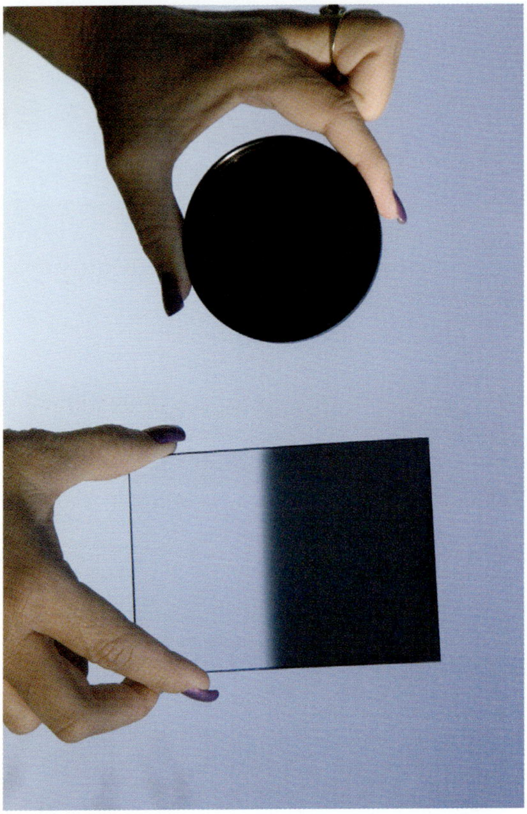

Figure 6.17 *Neutral-density filters, available in both graduated and solid versions, allow you to correct for extreme ranges of light that would not be recorded by a sensor.*

A graduated neutral density, or *grad*, is used to reduce the difference in light range between bright and shadow areas of a scene. In **Figure 6.18**, you can see that in order to capture detail in the ground, the sky details are blown out with very little detail.

Figure 6.18 *Without a filter, I've lost details in the sky in order to keep the ground from being too dark.*

Using a two-stop grad, I've darkened the sky by two stops without affecting the foreground at all, letting me capture more sky detail (**Figure 6.19**).

Figure 6.19 *With a two-stop graduated neutral-density filter, I can capture detail in both the sky and the ground.*

Tip

You can use a polarizer as a neutral-density filter, too. Doing so gives you as much as two stops of exposure latitude when adjusted for maximum effect.

The other type of neutral-density filter is solid and is used to extend the exposure for things like blurred water images (**Figure 6.20**). You can get these in different strengths. If you want to spend the money, the best one available is the Singh-Ray Vari-ND, which lets you adjust the strength like a polarizer filter.

Figure 6.20 *Using a solid neutral-density filter lets me slow the exposure down to get that soft, flowing look in the water.*

Special Effects in Image-Editing Programs

Although I would never go without my traditional filters, one of the nice advantages of shooting digital is the ability to use Photoshop and other image editors to enhance photos with special-effect filters that either mimic traditional photography filters or go beyond, doing things that could never be accomplished in the non-digital world.

Cross processing

If you ever shot film, especially slide film, you might be familiar with cross processing, either by choice or error. Cross processing is traditionally done by developing film in the wrong chemicals. As an example, if you were to develop negatives in E-6, or chrome chemicals, you'd be cross processing your negatives in a solution intended for slides. This has been a popular alternative way to develop film, and it's also possible to do the equivalent in the digital age. Now there are filters and plug-ins for Adobe Photoshop CS2 and Adobe Photoshop Elements that can accomplish the same goal of giving your images a new and different look, like what you see in **Figure 6.21**. PhotoKit Color 2.0 is a versatile plug-in suite produced by the good folks at PixelGenius (www.pixelgenius.com/color2/) that offers a cross-processing option along with many other creative filter techniques.

Figure 6.21 *Cross processing mimics the effect of developing film in the wrong chemicals.*

This type of effect works best (in my opinion) on landscape images where you want to give a slight otherworldly look to the scene.

Infrared

Although I can never see myself replacing my physical IR (infrared) filter for a purely digital solution, there are some impressive plug-ins available for Photoshop that let you convert your images to have an IR appearance. My favorite of these are the black-and-white and color IR conversion filters from Nik software (www.niksoftware.com). **Figure 6.22** shows a standard landscape photo with good greens, blue skies, but nothing particularly eye-catching to be seen.

Figure 6.22 *If you don't want to spring for an IR filter, there are software versions that can be used to create an IR effect. Here's the original image.*

By using the Nik Color Efex Infrared BW filter (**Figure 6.23**), I can choose from several default conversion methods, each of which is optimized for a different color range, and then fine-tune the highlights, brightness, and contrast until I get the image in **Figure 6.24**.

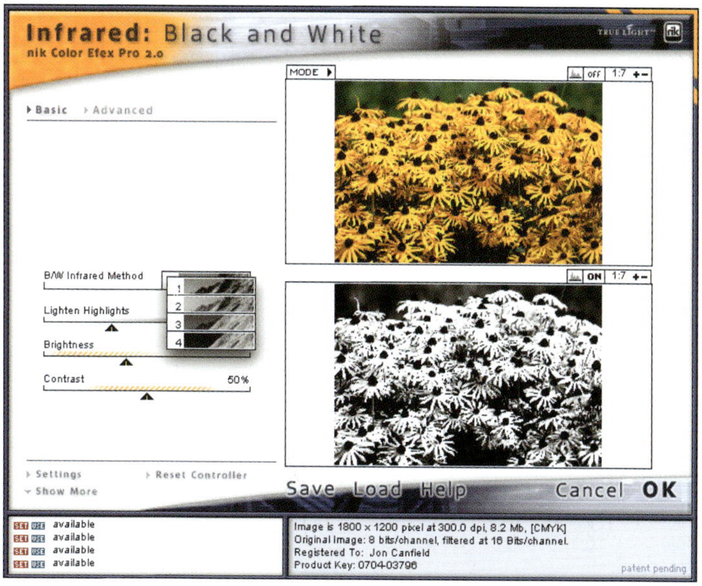

Figure 6.23 *Using the Nik Color Efex Infrared BW filter, I can select from different options to create an IR image.*

Figure 6.24 *Here's the final result after using the Nik filter to convert the image used in Figure 6.22.*

Using the Infrared Color filter gives the image a totally different feel by leaving the image in color but emphasizing a specific area of the color spectrum to create an image that just couldn't be captured by the naked eye (**Figure 6.25**).

Figure 6.25 *You can also get false color images by using an Infrared Color filter.*

Finally, I can choose an Infrared Thermal Camera filter for a true sci-fi look (**Figure 6.26**) or something that reminds the viewer of night-vision goggles.

Figure 6.26 *The Infrared Thermal Camera filter from Nik turns your image into one that looks like it was captured with a thermal sensor.*

Photo filters

Photoshop and Photoshop Elements come with sets of filters that mimic the traditional color, warming, and cooling filters that photographers have used for decades. Along with the common color filters like red, green, blue, yellow, and orange, Photoshop includes a variety of warming and cooling filters and some unusual ones, such as emerald green and underwater. You can also create your own from a color picker. To use these photo filters, select Layer > New Adjustment Layer > Photo Filter… (**Figure 6.27**).

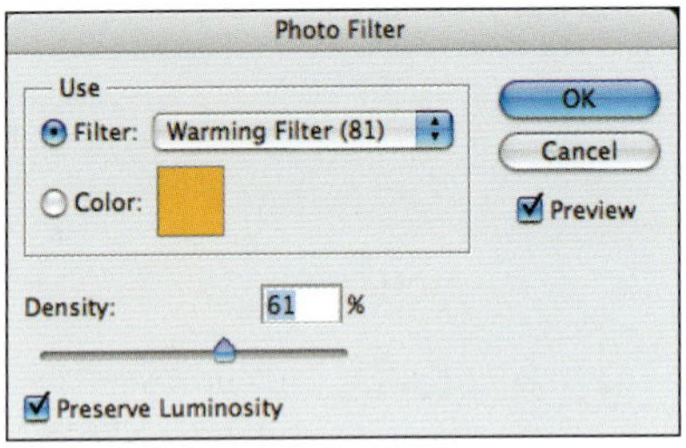

Figure 6.27 *Photo Filters, available in both Photoshop and Elements, offer a number of standard photo filters.*

To control how strong the effect is, adjust the Density slider below the preview window. I usually find that a density of 40-70% is best and have never needed to use 100%.

Black-and-white conversions

Black and white is going through a huge surge in popularity these days, with many cameras supporting black-and-white conversion directly in the camera. Unless you're shooting raw though, I highly recommend shooting in color mode to give you the most flexibility with your image files. You can always convert your images to black and white in an image-editing program on your computer, and you never know when you might want to use that photo in color someday.

In Photoshop Elements versions prior to 5.0, black-and-white conversion was limited to grayscale, which leaves quite a bit to be desired. Grayscale conversion is essentially just a desaturation of the image (**Figure 6.28**).

Photoshop CS2 users have the much more powerful Channel Mixer at their disposal, but along with power comes a bit of confusion. To use the Channel Mixer, select Layer > New Adjustment Layer > Channel Mixer… to open the dialog shown in **Figure 6.29**.

Figure 6.28 *A simple convert to grayscale doesn't do much for an image. There are better choices when you want to create a black-and-white photo.*

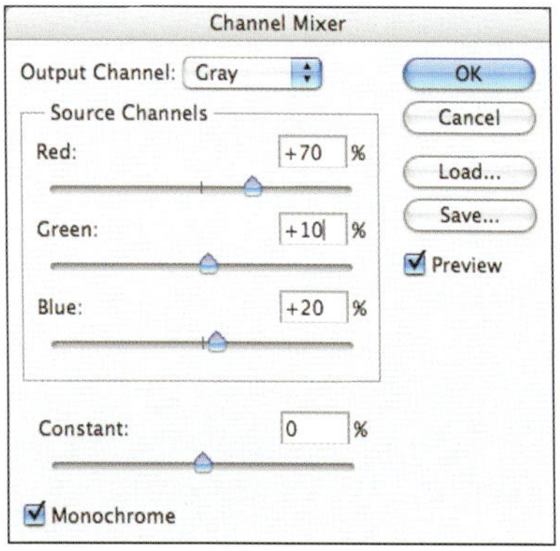

Figure 6.29 *Photoshop users have the Channel Mixer which gives much better results by letting you select each color channel separately.*

The first step is to click the Monochrome checkbox in the lower left corner, which converts your image to a grayscale look. The difference here is that all the color information is still in your photo, and you can adjust the individual color channels to emphasize different areas of the photo.

You want to keep the cumulative percentage of each color channel totalling 100% to maintain the overall exposure value. As an example, if I wanted to emphasize the clouds and darken the sky in a landscape image, I'd increase the Red channel, which has the effect of darkening blues. A positive value in each channel lightens that color and darkens its complementary color. For example, increasing the percentage of the Red channel lightens the reds and darkens the cyans. This darkens the values in the sky, which is predominantly cyan and blue. In **Figures 6.30a** through **6.30c**, you can see the effect of using each of the color channels at 100% and what the impact is on that color.

Figure 6.30a uses 100% red, **Figure 6.30b** uses 100% green, and **Figure 6.30c** uses 100% blue. Each shows a drastic difference in the areas of the image that are prominent. My final choice for this shot was a mix of 70% red, 20% green, and 10% blue, as shown in **Figure 6.31**.

Figure 6.30a *In this version, I have the Red channel at 100% with Green and Blue set to 0%.*

Figure 6.30b *Here the Green channel is set to 100% with Red and Blue set to 0%.*

Figure 6.30c *Finally, the Blue channel is at 100% with Red and Green at 0%. You can see how different each image looks depending on which channel you emphasize.*

Figure 6.31 *To come up with this image, I selected 70% Red, 20% Green, and 10% Blue. You should avoid going over 100% to prevent lost detail.*

Channel Mixer isn't the easiest tool to master, but its reputation for being overly complicated isn't really deserved. Still, if you don't want to spend a great deal of time learning the ins and outs of color channels, I highly recommend looking into one of the many available plug-ins, such as those from the already mentioned Nik software (niksoftware.com) and PixelGenius's excellent PhotoKit collection (www.pixelgenius.com) (**Figure 6.32**).

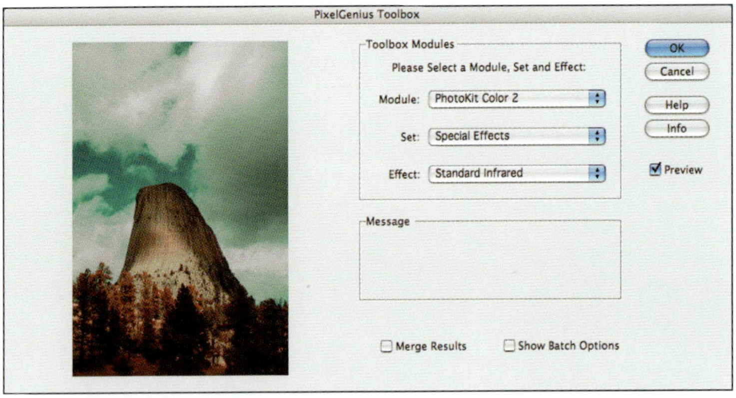

Figure 6.32 *PhotoKit from PixelGenius is one of the best tools available for making color adjustments in Photoshop.*

These filters and actions have a number of presets that allow you to quickly reproduce classic black-and-white effects, including high-contrast film with grain (**Figure 6.33**), sepia toning (**Figure 6.34**), and alternative processing like platinum or selenium which have been very popular with fine art photographers for years (**Figure 6.35**). These final three figures were all done with the PixelGenius PhotoKit plug-in.

Figure 6.33 *It's easy to simulate alternative-processing looks. Here, I've added grain to simulate fast black-and-white film.*

Figure 6.34 *Sepia tone is a popular choice for a vintage look.*

Figure 6.35 *Selenium toning is another choice for monochromatic images.*

7 Working with Raw Files

Raw file support isn't limited to digital SLR cameras, but all dSLR cameras include raw image capture. And while most dSLR camera manufacturers also include conversion software, by far the most popular converter is Adobe Photoshop Camera Raw, part of Photoshop Elements and Photoshop CS2.

I touch on the major conversion options here, but the bulk of this chapter is devoted to helping you get the most from your camera and Camera Raw.

The Buzz Over Raw

Raw is a hot topic, and most advanced digital cameras now support raw capture. What is the benefit to shooting in raw formats, and why choose raw over JPEG? What tools are available for working with raw images? In our first lesson, we'll take a look at the advantages of raw and the basic workflow of getting ready for converting raw images into files that can be edited by Photoshop or Photoshop Elements.

The raw image format captures the basic exposure data recorded by the camera's sensor without any additional processing applied. Your dSLR camera has a number of options that affect what happens to the image after capture. White balance settings, sharpening, noise reduction, and color balance are the primary adjustments. Actually, every photo you take with a digital camera is a raw file. The difference is that when you shoot in JPEG, all of the processing is done in the camera immediately after the capture. When you shoot in raw, the exposure settings are saved with the file but not actually applied to it, giving you the opportunity to make changes later on to the raw file.

This makes it sound like raw is the perfect format, doesn't it? In many cases it is. After all, you want control over how your photos look, and the extra flexibility is hard to beat. There are times when shooting raw isn't the best choice, though, such as event photography where you might be doing on-site printing—think Little League games, prom photos, and school photos, for example. Here the goal is to quickly take the photo and output a print, perhaps with no computer present. You certainly don't want to invest the time to edit several hundred images on the spot. Photo journalism is another area where raw is not a good choice. Most news services have specific guidelines on how to submit images—JPEG only, certain compression and sharpening settings, and so on.

Every digital camera that supports a raw format includes some form of conversion software, ranging from the very good to the barely adequate. Photoshop CS2 and Photoshop Elements 4.0 users have one of the best raw converters included with the program: Adobe Camera Raw. But, because Photoshop isn't the program for everyone, I also look at other converters, including the ones included with Canon and Nikon cameras.

Renaming Files

Before you can start working with your raw files, you need to get them onto your computer. This is the first step in your workflow, and taking the time to do things in a standardized way will make life easier.

Establishing a standard naming system will do more to help the initial workflow than almost anything else you can do. The name your camera assigns to an image is less than intuitive. Imagine browsing through thousands of images with names like _E7U2349.CR2 or DCS22893.NEF and you can easily see the benefit of giving your images more understandable and memorable names.

Luckily, Photoshop CS2 and Photoshop Elements 5.0 both make the renaming process painless. Photoshop Elements 5.0 running on a Windows PC has a Rename function that can be found in the Organizer (**Figure 7.1**). If you're using Photoshop CS2, or Elements on the Mac, go to the Adobe Bridge feature and select Tools > Batch Rename to display a dialog box like the one shown in **Figure 7.2**.

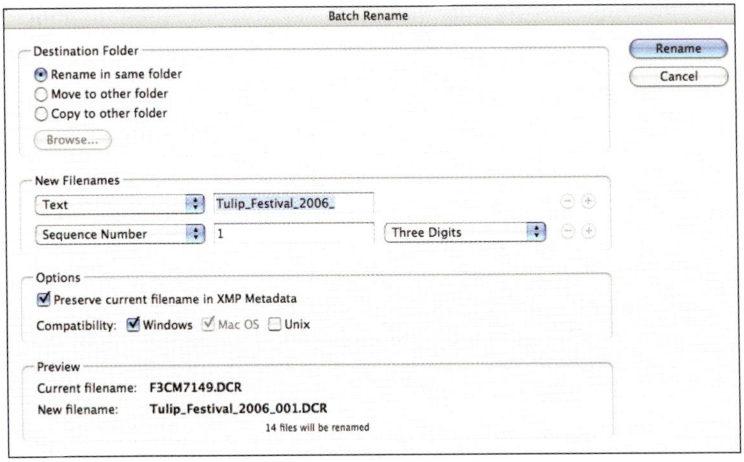

Figure 7.1 *Photoshop Elements Organizer on Windows has a Rename function that works with multiple files.*

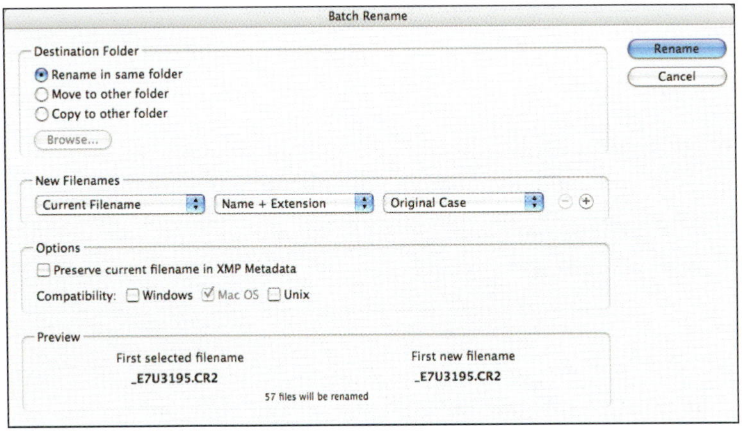

Figure 7.2 *Photoshop CS2 and Mac users of Elements have a more powerful batch rename function in Bridge.*

When renaming images you have the option to rename the file in the same folder or to move the renamed file to a new folder. Unless you have a good reason, I recommend selecting "Rename in same folder" in the Destination box. In the New Filenames box there are numerous naming parameters available in the top drop-down option box. I select the Text option since I normally use the subject and date as the filename, along with a three- or four-digit sequence number. The bottom drop-down option can be set to Sequence Number, with the second field set to a desired starting number (in this case 1) and the third field set to the desired number of digits. When the Rename button in the top right corner of the dialog box is clicked, the files are renamed and numbered sequentially.

For example, if I have a set of images that were shot in Yosemite, all the images will be renamed starting with yosemite_20050627_001. CR2_. Yosemite is the subject, the images are from June 27, 2005, and 001 would be the image's three-digit sequential number. The CR2 at the end designates the file format. Batch rename shows an example of the filename at the bottom of the dialog box (**Figure 7.3**).

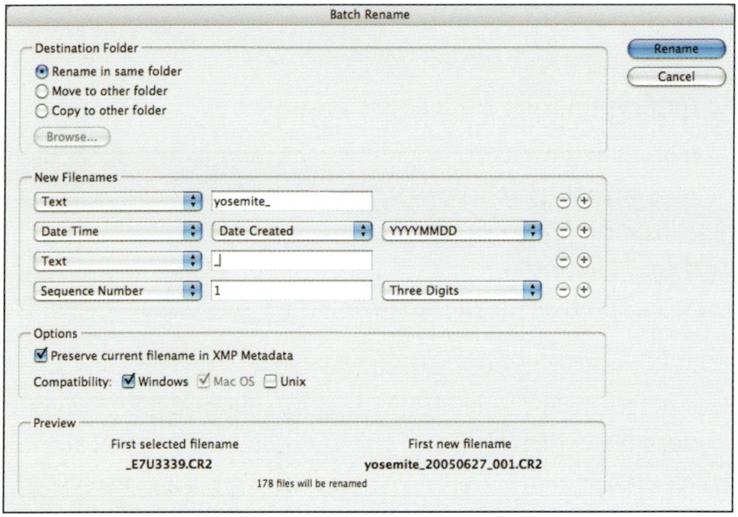

Figure 7.3 *Use meaningful names and sequence numbers to help identify images quickly.*

Tagging Files

The next step in the raw workflow is tagging your images for future editing. Using keywords that make sense to you and using the rating features in your image browser will help you quickly locate the files you want to convert (**Figure 7.4**).

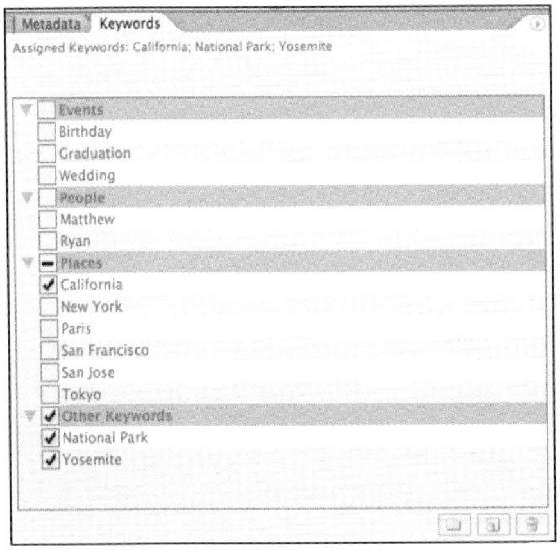

Figure 7.4 *Keywords and ratings can help you quickly sort and find images that match your needs.*

Selecting images for conversion

Wouldn't it be great if every image we took was perfect and worthy of printing or sharing? It would certainly save time and effort. After all, if all our shots were perfect, we'd probably take fewer photos. And, we'd know up front that every photo we took was going to be converted from raw to TIFF for touchup and other work.

Because every image isn't perfect, many serious photographers tend to shoot many variations of the same subject. Slight changes to composition, depth of field, and other creative aspects of an image are common and result in a large number of files to review.

Selecting by keyword

If you've been diligent about assigning keywords, or *tags*, to your images as you add them to your collection, the easiest way to select images for further processing is by keyword selection. For the following lessons, I'll be using Adobe Bridge (**Figure 7.5**), which is part of Photoshop CS2 on Mac and Windows and the Macintosh version of Elements; and Adobe Organizer (**Figure 7.6**), which is part of the Windows version of Elements.

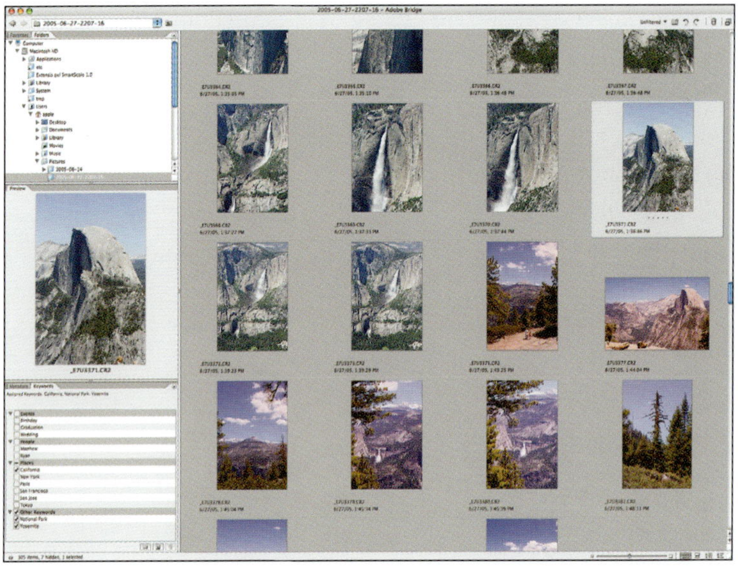

Figure 7.5 *Keywording in Bridge is done in the Keywords Panel shown here.*

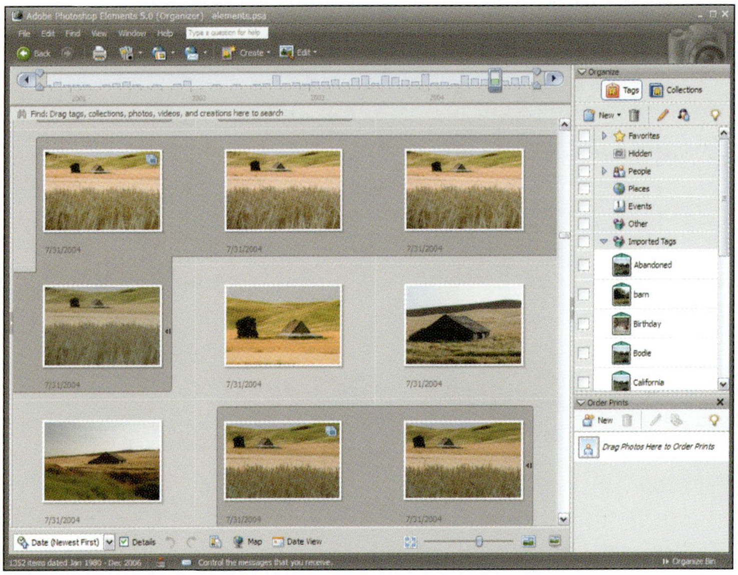

Figure 7.6 *Organizer, included with the Windows version of Elements, uses tags, which are the same as keywords.*

In Bridge, keywords can be searched by clicking Edit > Find in the option bar to bring up the Find dialog box. By clicking the + button in the Criteria field, up to 13 search fields can be used utilizing 11 different criteria. One of these criteria is Keywords. For example, the search shown in **Figure 7.7** will only find images that contain *Luke* and *Clay* as keywords if the "If all criteria are met" option is selected in the Match window at the bottom of the Find dialog box.

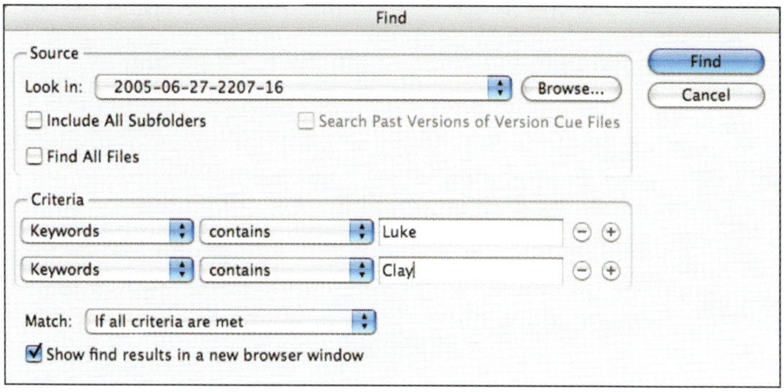

Figure 7.7 *You can combine keywords to find multiple items by using AND to find all images that include both keywords.*

If *Clay* is removed from the search, then all images that contain *Luke* will be returned (**Figure 7.8**).

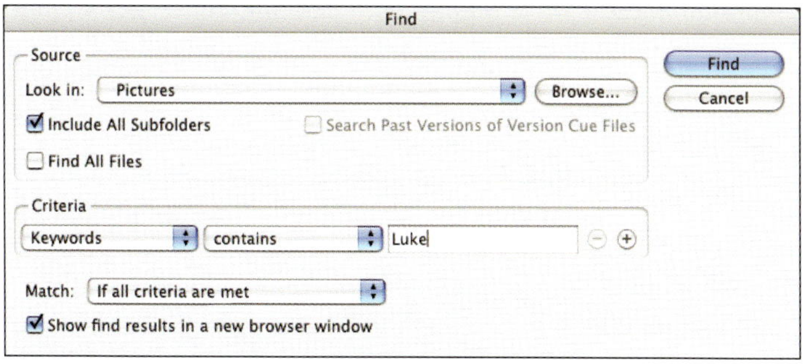

Figure 7.8 *You can refine a search by modifying the criteria. Here, I've removed Clay and only the images containing Luke are shown.*

Bridge has quite a bit more flexibility in its search settings. To change the matching requirements, select "If any criteria are met."

This will find and display any images that have the keywords *Luke* or *Clay*, as shown in **Figure 7.9**.

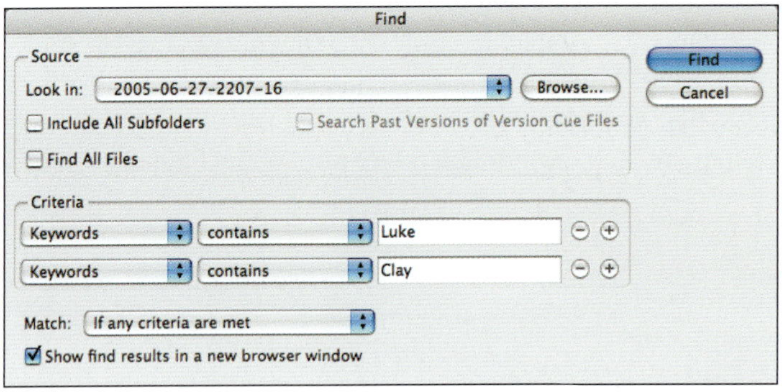

Figure 7.9 *Unlike AND, using OR finds all images that have either keyword.*

The Bridge search dialog also lets you specify other criteria to search by, including by Rating or Label (**Figure 7.10**).

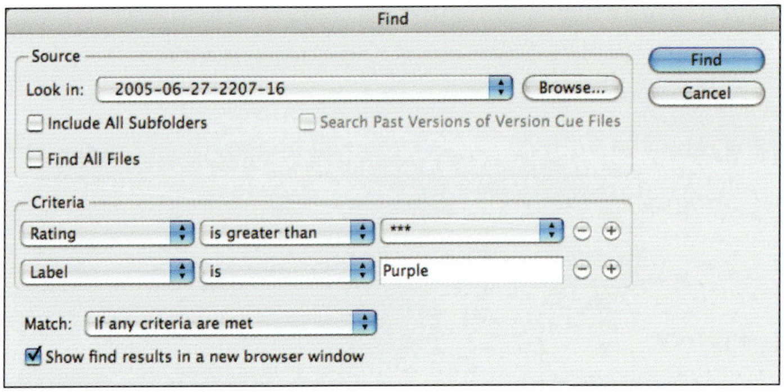

Figure 7.10 *In Bridge you can also search by ratings or labels.*

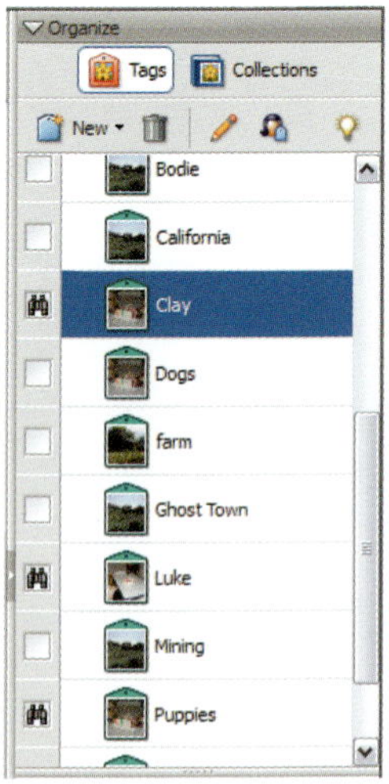

Figure 7.11 *Organizer provides a very visual method of selecting tags for search queries.*

Organizer uses a system that is a bit different—one that I have a love-hate relationship with. Rather than using a Search dialog, you simply check the boxes next to the tags, or keywords, that you want to find. I love the simplicity of this method. Clicking one or more tags allows you to build a complex selection without much effort (**Figure 7.11**). The hate part of my relationship comes when I'm trying to locate the desired tags from a large collection of icons in the Tag window.

In the example shown in **Figure 7.12**, the tags selected for searching are shown with a binocular icon.

Figure 7.12 *When you've selected tags for searching, a binocular is shown with the tag as a visual reminder.*

Multiple tag selections work as an "and" search parameter. In this example, Organizer would find only those images that were tagged with *Kathy, Ken, Erin, Bo, Rose, Clay,* and *Luke*. It's not likely that many images would contain all of these tags, so you can modify the search to perform like an OR by clicking the Close checkbox above the thumbnails as I've done here in **Figure 7.13**.

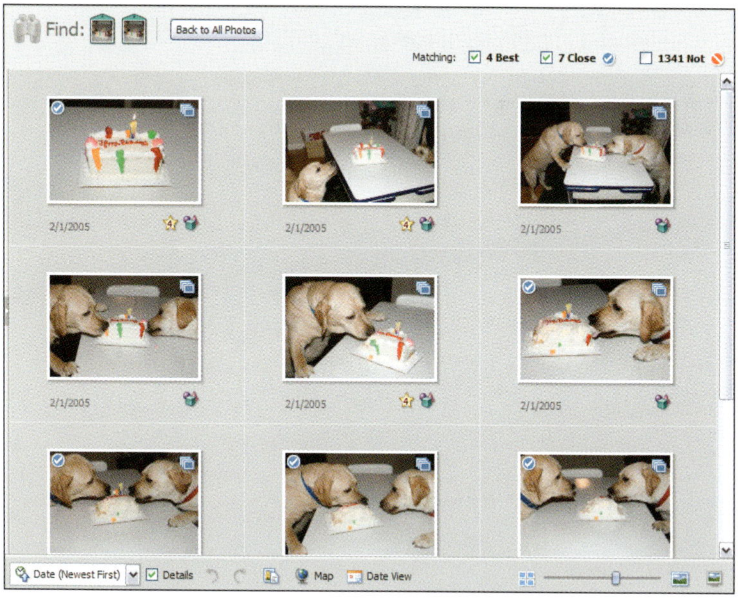

Figure 7.13 *By default, multiple tags work as an AND, but you can modify this by clicking the Close checkbox.*

In addition to selecting directly from tags, there are a wealth of options available in the Find menu that are useful for finding images. In particular, selecting by date range and History comes in handy to only show images within a particular set of dates, or images that you have submitted or used previously (**Figure 7.14**).

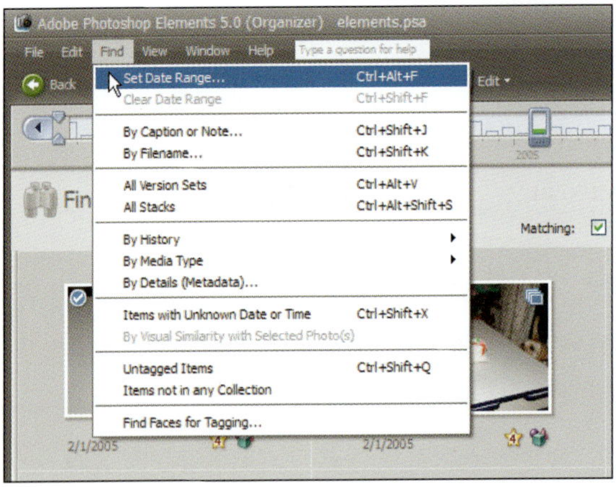

Figure 7.14 *Organizer also includes a number of options to select by date, history, or even location on a map.*

Selecting by rating

Organizer, Bridge, and iPhoto users can also select by rating. If you have a large group of similar images, it can be effective to make a selection based on keywords and then narrow down the results by using ratings. In Bridge, this can be done as part of the search by adding a Rating criteria, as seen in **Figure 7.15**.

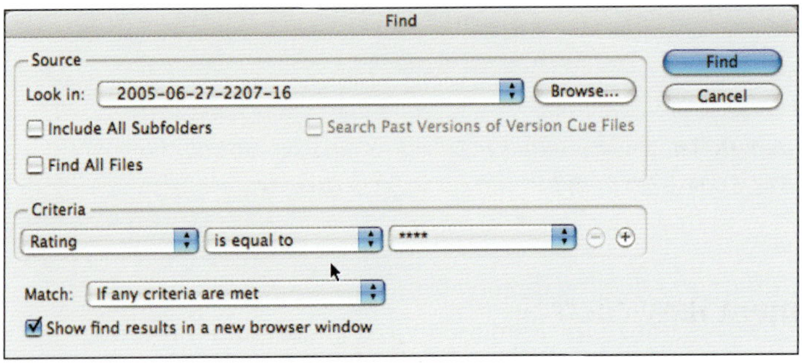

Figure 7.15 *All of the image organizers include a rating feature to help identify the best images. In Bridge, you can use this in a search criteria.*

Figure 7.16 *A second use of the ratings or labels in Bridge is to filter a selection of images after running a query by selecting the appropriate option from the Filter list.*

Alternatively, you can narrow down the selection after the search by selecting the rating or label from the Filter list at the top of the Bridge thumbnail view, as shown in **Figure 7.16**.

Rating selections in Organizer are done the same way as other tags. Clicking the box next to the Rating tag selects all images with that rating. To select more than one rating level, click each rating tag you want. For example, selecting the 4 Stars and 3 Stars tags shows all images that are rated at 3 or 4, as shown in **Figure 7.17**.

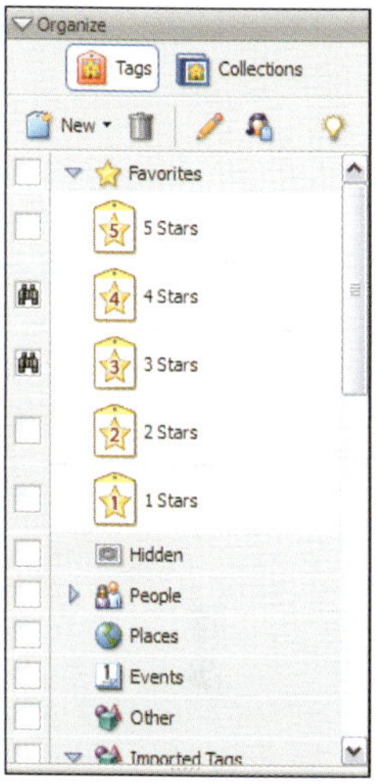

Figure 7.17 *Like other tags in Organizer, you simply click on the rating you want to search by.*

Camera Raw Basics

Now that we have basic tagging covered, let's jump in with an overview of Camera Raw, which is shown in **Figure 7.18**.

Figure 7.18 *The Camera Raw converter, seen here in the Photoshop CS2 version, is one of the most popular converters available.*

Camera Raw controls

Before we begin making adjustments, let's take a look at the Camera Raw interface. The Preview area is used for overall previews of all the editing operations you'll be performing on the raw image prior to conversion. Because Photoshop Elements and Photoshop have different tools, I cover each of them separately.

The large Preview area is where you'll see the effect of changes made to the various slider controls when you have the Preview checkbox enabled. And there is really no point in using Camera Raw without Preview enabled—after all, how will you know what the adjustments are doing without previewing?

Two of the most helpful options for Preview are the Shadow and Highlight checkboxes, shown in **Figure 7.19**. With these turned on, you can see when image data is being *clipped*, or lost. Shadow clipping is shown as blue, and highlight clipping is red. As you make adjustments to the Exposure, Shadows, Brightness, and Contrast sliders, you can see when you've hit the limit for a control by looking for these clipping warnings.

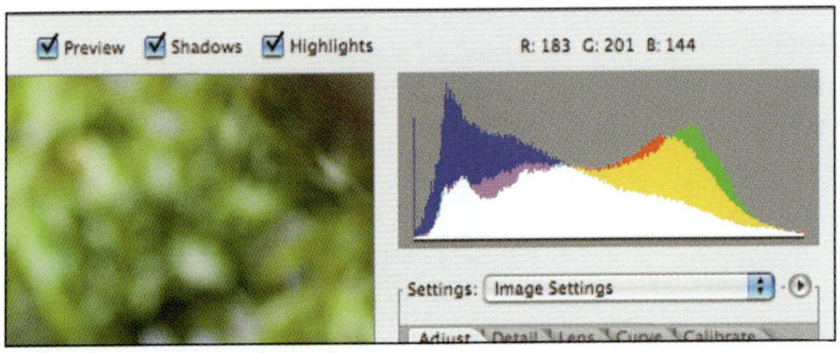

Figure 7.19 *By checking the Shadow and Highlight preview checkboxes, you can see areas of your image that have exposure problems.*

Below the Preview area are different controls based on which version of Camera Raw you're using. Both versions include a drop-down list box to change the size of your preview, helpful when you want to focus on a critical area of your image when making adjustments. Both also include a drop-down for the bit depth your image will be converted at, with choices for 8 bit or 16 bit. I prefer to do all my conversion at 16 bit, but for most uses, 8 bit will work fine. In fact, if you use Elements, very few editing options are available for 16-bit files, so you're just as well off converting at 8 bit to start with.

Elements users will also see the Shadow and Highlight clipping checkboxes along with the Rotate tools (**Figure 7.20**).

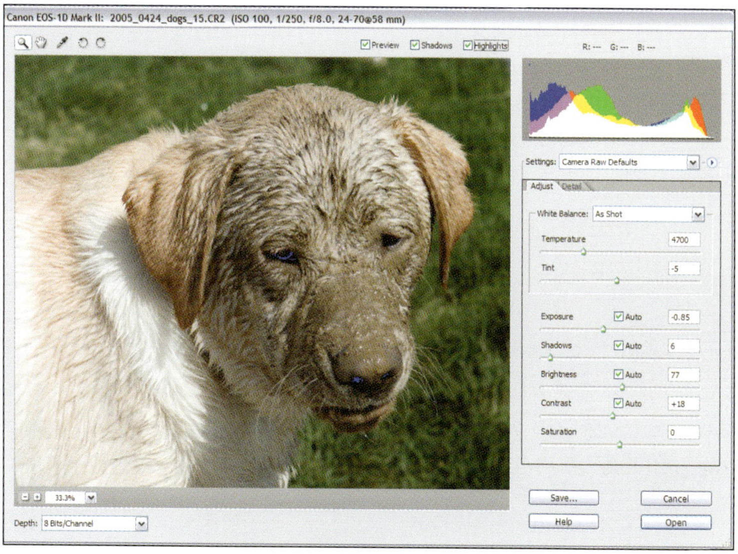

Figure 7.20 *The version of Camera Raw included with Elements is essentially the same, but does include fewer options.*

Figure 7.21 *Along with the Rotate tools, Photoshop CS2 adds Crop, Straighten, and Color Sampler to the Camera Raw toolbar.*

Toolbars

Both Elements and Photoshop CS2 have several toolbar icons for common tasks. Elements has tools for magnifying the preview, moving the area displayed in the Preview window, and selecting white balance. CS2 includes these tools and adds a Crop tool, Straighten tool, Color Sampler, and the Rotate tools (**Figure 7.21**).

The Crop tool and Straighten tool are perhaps the most useful of the tools in Camera Raw, letting you work on just the portion of your image that you want without making a destructive or permanent change to the original raw image file. You can drag out a crop of any size, or use one of the preset options (**Figure 7.22**) to crop your image to a specific size. When the image is converted, only the cropped portion is opened as a new document in Photoshop. The crop can be changed or cleared at any time in the raw file for different uses of the same image.

Figure 7.22 *Cropping in Camera Raw is useful when you know that you don't need all of the image area in your conversion. And unlike cropping in Photoshop, it's non-destructive in Camera Raw, so you can change your mind at any time.*

The Straighten tool works similarly to the Crop tool. By dragging out a line that should be straight—either horizontal or vertical—

> **Note**
>
> Just as in Photoshop, in Camera Raw you can hold the spacebar down to activate the Move tool.

Camera Raw automatically creates a crop with the maximum possible size and already rotated to straighten the image (**Figure 7.23**).

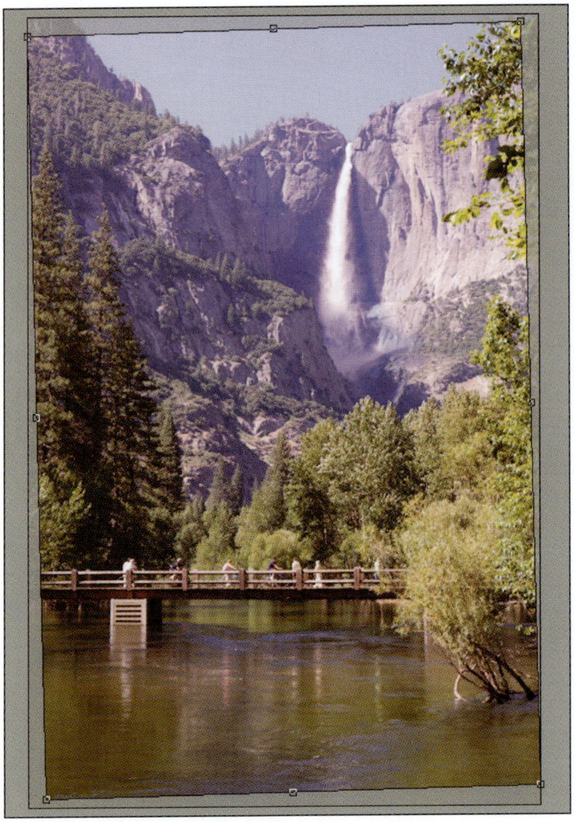

Figure 7.23 *Straighten performs two tasks. First, it lets you fix any tilts you have in your image, and then it crops the image to the maximum size possible based on the new horizon.*

The Adjustment Sliders

The controls on the first tab, Adjust, are common to both versions of Camera Raw—the one in Elements and the one included with Photoshop CS2. The screen shown in **Figure 7.24** is from Photoshop CS2 and includes the new Auto settings for exposure, shadows, brightness, and contrast.

White balance will be set to whatever setting was used in the camera at the time of capture. When shooting raw, I leave white balance set to Auto because I know that I can easily change it in the converter. If you've ever set your white balance to "daylight" and then shot indoors, the results of which are shown in Figure 7.24, you'll immediately understand the value of being able to change the setting in Camera Raw.

Figure 7.24 *Shooting with the wrong white balance setting can be difficult to correct unless you're shooting in raw, where a simple adjustment saves the day.*

There are presets for most of the common white balance settings, and by adjusting the Temperature and Tint sliders, you can create your own custom white balance. Higher temperature numbers add a yellow cast to the image, warming it up, whereas lower numbers add a blue cast, cooling the image down. Daylight is about 5500, but many people find that moving this up to 5700 gives the effect of using a warming filter on their images. The Tint slider shifts the color balance of the image. Moving the slider to the right adds magenta, and moving to the left adds green, allowing you to fine-tune the color in your image (**Figure 7.25**).

Figure 7.25 The Tint sliders are used to fine-tune your color balance by adding green or magenta to the image.

When none of the preset options work, it's time to select the eyedropper from the toolbar. By clicking on a neutral area of your image, you can correct for a colorcast that can then be fine-tuned by making adjustments to the Temperature and Tint sliders, as shown in **Figure 7.26**.

Figure 7.26 Here's the same image I used in Figure 7.24 corrected for color balance by selecting the closest preset temperature and then fine-tuning the adjustment.

Before looking at each slider, I want to add a note on the Auto settings. In many cases, Auto works very well for your images. Camera Raw does an amazing job of analyzing the image to get the best settings. It's not always right, but it often gets you very close to where you want to be. Any adjustment of a slider turns Auto off for that slider. Clicking the checkbox resets the control to where Camera Raw thinks it should be. You can toggle all of the Auto checkboxes on or off by pressing Ctrl+U (Command+U on Macintosh).

Exposure slider

The Exposure slider lets you make adjustments of up to four f-stops in either direction. Under normal circumstances, you don't want to make huge changes here, especially to correct for under-exposure. Adding more than two stops of exposure starts to show obvious noise problems. These can be corrected to some extent with the Luminance Smoothing and Color Noise Reduction sliders, but you'll see some softening of the image when using these controls. As always, proper exposure when capturing the image is your best bet for a quality image, but when mistakes happen, the Exposure adjustment control can be your friend.

Now for the first of those helpful hints on making image adjustments. Along with the Shadow and Highlight clipping checkboxes, you can set the entire Preview area to show clipping when making adjustments to the Exposure slider. Hold down the Alt (Mac Option) key while making adjustments to the Exposure slider. The Preview area will turn black, as seen in **Figure 7.27**. As you drag the slider to the right, you see parts of your image display. Everything that shows up here are highlight areas that will be clipped (**Figure 7.28**). This is an easier way to see when data is being clipped than the red and blue indicators in the shadow/highlight clipping warnings because all other tonal values are hidden from view.

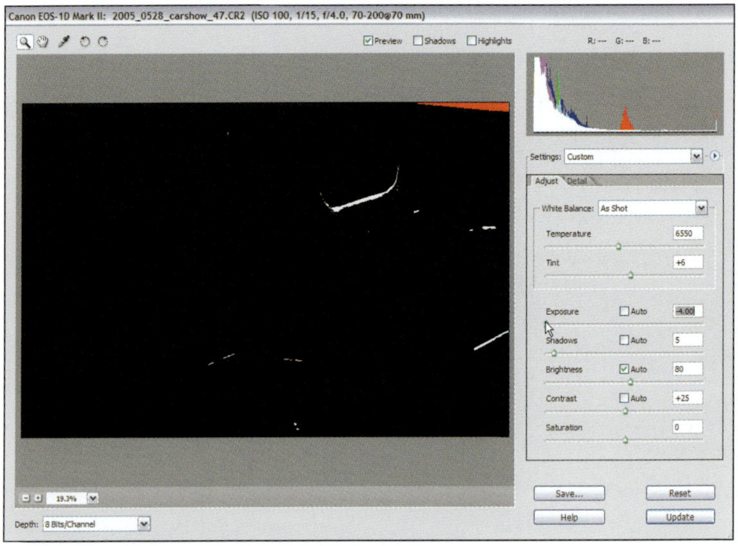

Figure 7.27 *Holding down the Alt key (Windows) or Option key (Mac) while moving the Exposure slider turns the entire Preview area into a clipping warning. If the Preview is all black, everything is within range on the highlights. When you start to see white, you know that you've adjusted the exposure to a level that will lose some highlight information.*

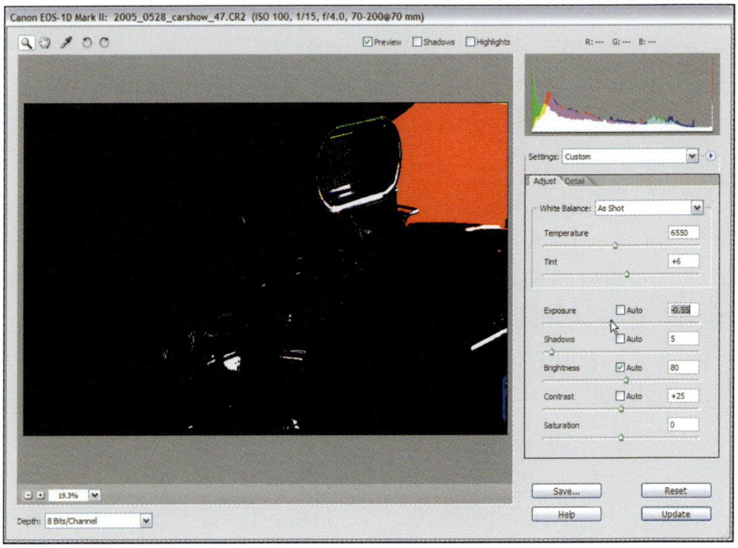

Figure 7.28 *This is an example of an image that has the exposure adjusted too much and is losing highlight details.*

Shadows slider

The Shadows slider controls where the deepest shadow areas of your image will be. Like the Exposure slider, holding down the Alt (Mac Option) key turns the entire Preview area into a clipping area (**Figure 7.29**). The preview turns white, and as you increase the Shadows slider you see portions of your image begin to display. Anything showing here as black will be rendered totally black in your converted image.

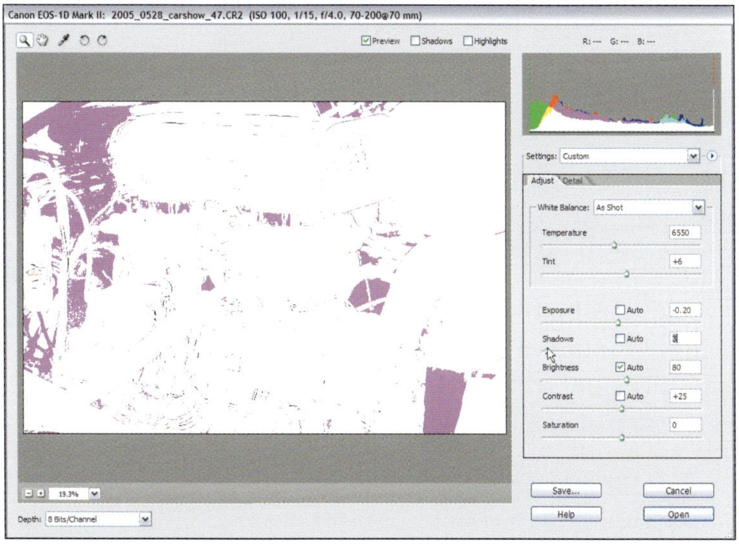

Figure 7.29 *Like the Exposure slider, holding down Alt or Option while adjusting the Shadows slider gives you a large Preview area to show shadow clipping. Here, the Preview is all white until you begin to lose shadow detail.*

Brightness slider

The Brightness slider controls the overall brightness for your image, with higher numbers lightening the entire image, and lower numbers darkening it. This control, as well as the Contrast slider (covered next), work best when used with the histogram. You'll want to watch the histogram data move as you adjust the Brightness slider and avoid having the histogram data block up on the right side, indicating that highlight data is being lost (**Figure 7.30**).

Figure 7.30 *The Brightness slider is used along with the Histogram display to change the overall brightness of your image.*

Contrast slider

Like the Brightness slider, Contrast controls where the midtones in your image are (**Figure 7.31**). Settings higher than 25 add more contrast by darkening the values below the midtone and lighting those above the midtone. Settings below 25 reduce contrast by lightening values below the midtone and darkening values above it.

Figure 7.31 *The Contrast slider controls the midtones in the image. Higher settings (above 25) add more contrast, and lower values lighten the colors below the midtone.*

Saturation slider

A simple word of advice here. Unless you're going for a special effect such as monochrome conversions or toning, which I cover later in the chapter, don't make adjustments to saturation in Camera Raw. This is best left for post-conversion in Photoshop, where you have more control over how the saturation is modified.

The Details Tab

The final three controls shared by all versions of Camera Raw are Sharpening, Luminance Smoothing, and Color Noise Reduction. These controls are found by switching to the Details tab in Camera Raw (**Figure 7.32**).

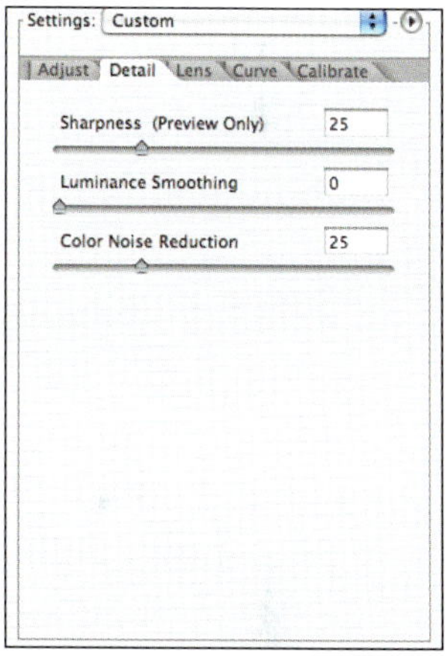

Figure 7.32 *The Details tab has controls for sharpening and noise reduction.*

Sharpening

Every digital image needs sharpening. It doesn't matter how good the lens is, what your technique is, or what the resolution of the camera is. Most digital cameras use an anti-aliasing filter to reduce moiré in the captured image. This filter adds softness to your images which, when you shoot JPEG, is removed as part of the image processing done by the camera. Camera Raw includes a Sharpness control that lets you add or adjust sharpness as part of the conversion process. There's only one problem with this—sharpening should be the last step in your digital workflow!

The settings used to sharpen an image are very different for a Web shot vs. a 4 x 6 print, vs. an 8 x 10 print. Each has special needs, and applying sharpening now, before you've done your other image edits, results in a lower-quality final product. Photoshop CS2 users of Camera Raw can set sharpening to be active only for the preview. When you convert your image, any sharpening that has been applied is ignored in the converted file. To activate this feature, click the small triangle next to the Settings list and select Preferences. Now select "Preview images only" from the "Apply sharpening to:" list, as shown in **Figure 7.33**. The slider label updates to show that sharpness settings are applied to preview only.

Note

This preview-only sharpening option isn't available for Elements users. If you use the Sharpness slider, you need to remember to set it back to 0 before converting.

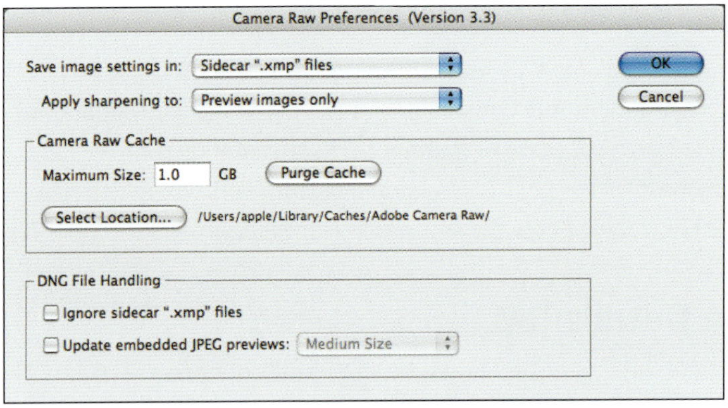

Figure 7.33 *The Photoshop CS2 version of Camera Raw allows you to set the sharpening to be used only on the preview, which I recommend. Elements users need to adjust the slider to zero before converting.*

In Photoshop Elements 5.0 using sharpening in Camera Raw is helpful because you have a better idea of what the processed image will look like, but remember to turn it off before actually converting your image!

Luminance Smoothing

The Luminance Smoothing control corrects one type of noise in your image. Typically seen in dense shadow areas, and more obvious with high ISO or long exposure images, luminance noise resembles the grain you see in traditional film.

Because any adjustments made to this control introduce some image softness, it's critical to work with your Preview area zoomed in as much as possible to the critical area that you're trying to correct. I often work at 300% zoom when making adjustments (**Figure 7.34**).

Tip

Use the up and down arrow keys on your keyboard to adjust the slider one increment at a time.

Here is one of the times that using the Sharpness slider can be helpful to you. Increasing sharpness makes the noise patterns more obvious in your image, letting you see how your corrections are being applied.

Typically, only small adjustments to luminance smoothing are needed. I very seldom go above 10, and any setting above 15-20

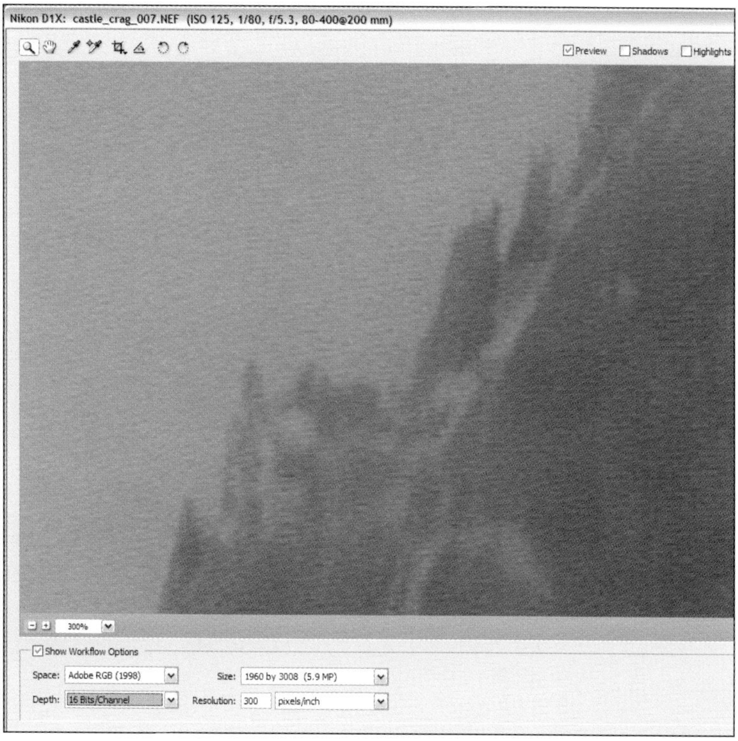

Figure 7.34 *Zoom up to 300% in your Preview area to see the adjustments in the area you are trying to correct.*

would be very rare indeed. In the example shown in **Figure 7.35a**, I can see a fair amount of noise, especially in the clouds above the mountains. If needed, I can zoom in on the problem areas for a closer look and increase the Sharpness slider to make the noise more obvious.

Making small adjustments to the Luminance Smoothing slider, I reduce the noise to acceptable levels with a setting of 8, as shown in **Figure 7.35b**. The photo in **Figure 7.36** shows a more common luminance correction.

Figure 7.35a Luminance noise resembles film grain and is most obvious in shadow areas. Working at high magnifications makes it easier to see and adjust.

Figure 7.35b Here's the result of using luminance smoothing on the previous image. Notice that the grainy appearance is much less obvious now.

Figure 7.36 Here's a more typical example of luminance smoothing that requires a setting of 8 to correct.

Color noise reduction

If you have green or magenta spots in your images, you've been attacked by color noise. It's especially obvious around highlights and in shadow areas of your images. Long exposure and high ISO settings that make the sensor more sensitive to heat are the main culprits here, and it's easy to see the problem in the example shown in **Figure 7.37**.

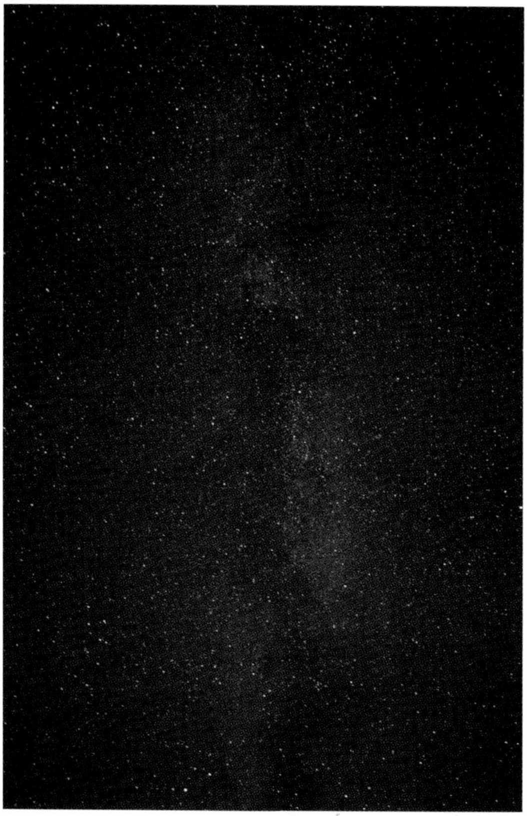

Figure 7.37 *Color noise is a problem when shooting long exposures or at high ISO settings, but it's much better than the same image shot with a compact camera and smaller sensor.*

The method of correcting color noise is very similar to that used for luminance smoothing. Start off by zooming in as much as needed to see detail in the problem area of your image.

Although correcting color noise doesn't soften your image the same way that luminance smoothing does, you still want to keep adjustments to a minimum to avoid changing other areas of your image.

The image I'm using in Figure 7.37 is an extreme example but shows just how much you can recover. If I had shot this as a JPEG, I would have just deleted it immediately. I typically start at the default setting of 25 and work my way up from there, keeping a close eye in the Preview area of the portion of the image showing the worst noise problem. In the example shown here, a setting of 42 did the best job of reducing noise (**Figure 7.38**).

Figure 7.38 *Using the Color Noise slider at a setting of 42 has cleaned up the image shown in Figure 7.37.*

Other noise-reduction options

There are better tools available for reducing noise than those included in Camera Raw. When you have problems that you just can't clean up with Camera Raw, it's time to look to one of these options.

Noise Ninja (www.picturecode.com), Nik Dfine (www.nikmultimedia.com), and Neat Image (www.neatimage.com) all do a very good job and have loyal followings. My personal favorite is Noiseware (www.imagenomic.com), which is amazing in both the quality of the cleanup, and in the way it learns how your camera records noise—actually giving you better results with more image samples (**Figure 7.39**).

Figure 7.39 *To be honest, when I have noise issues I normally turn to Noiseware from Imagenomic—it does an incredible job much more easily than I could.*

The Lens Tab

The Lens tab contains controls to adjust chromatic aberration, which is commonly seen along the edges of bright areas. The two sliders control either red and cyan or blue and yellow fringing. By moving the sliders to the left, you'll remove either red or blue from the image, while adjustments to the right will correct for cyan or yellow problems, as shown in **Figure 7.40**.

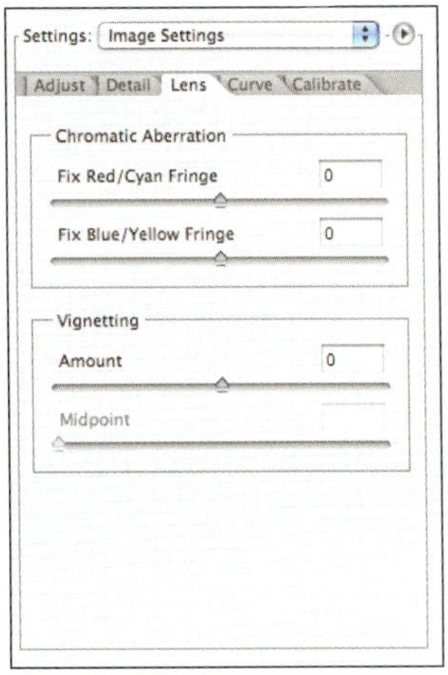

Figure 7.40 *The Lens tab, only in the Photoshop CS2 version of Camera Raw, includes controls to correct chromatic aberration and vignetting in your digital images.*

__Figure 7.41a__ Wide-angle lenses, especially with filters, can lead to darkening or vignetting at the corners.

__Figure 7.41b__ Using the Vignette control you can remove or greatly reduce the amount of vignetting in the shot.

The Vignetting control can correct for darkening seen at the edges of images with some lenses (**Figures 7.41a** and **7.41b**). An alternative use for the control is to add vignetting to draw attention to the center of your image. The Midpoint slider controls how far from the center of the image the vignetting adjustments occur (**Figure 7.42**).

Figure 7.42 *An alternate use of the Vignette control is to add vignetting to the image, darkening the corners to draw more attention to the center of the photo.*

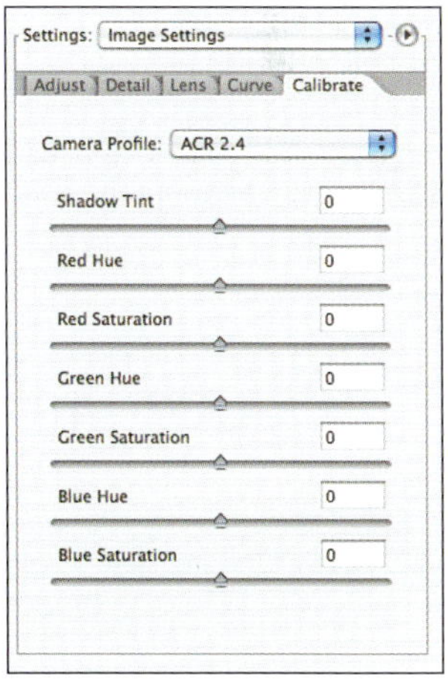

Figure 7.43 *The Calibrate tab, also only available with the Photoshop CS2 version of Camera Raw, has adjustment sliders to color balance, similar to the Channel Mixer in Photoshop.*

The Calibrate Tab

The controls on the Calibrate tab (**Figure 7.43**) adjust for color balance in a fashion similar to using the Channel Mixer in Photoshop. Shadow Tint controls the overall tone of the image, with adjustments to the left adding green and adjustments to the right adding magenta to the image. The remaining controls affect each color channel to increase or decrease the amount and intensity of that color.

When used with the Saturation slider on the Adjust tab, you can create monochrome images with enhanced tone, similar to using a color filter with black and white film, as seen in **Figure 7.44**.

Figure 7.44 *Combined with the Saturation control, you can use the Shadow Tint and color controls to create toned monochrome images.*

Note

You can find detailed information on using curves and other advanced conversion controls in my book *Raw 101: Better Images with Photoshop and Photoshop Elements.*

The Curve Tab

The Curve tab (**Figure 7.45**) is new to Photoshop CS2. Like the curve control in Photoshop, you can use it to adjust the black and white points and midtones of your image.

Although I prefer to make adjustments to curves within Photoshop, the control is useful for adding quick contrast settings with the presets above the histogram.

Some of the more useful options in the curve control are the presets for different tone curves, which can help to quickly check different settings for the optimal conversion results. Linear (**Figure 7.46**) does no adjustment to the curves, Medium (**Figure 7.47**) boosts contrast slightly and is a good choice for many image types, and Strong (**Figure 7.48**) is a more obvious adjustment that accentuates shadow detail. Finally, Custom is displayed when you make manual adjustments to the curve.

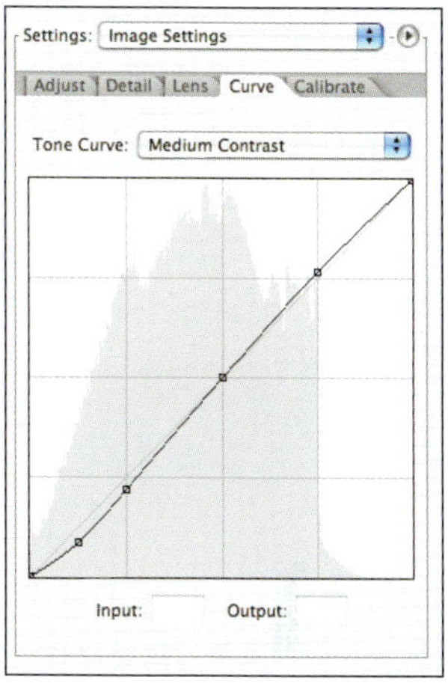

Figure 7.45 *The Curve tab, available only in the Photoshop CS2 version, works very similar to the Curves command in Photoshop, but adds two nice features by including the histogram in the display and coming with preset curves for different image types.*

Figure 7.46 *Using a Linear curve, which is the default and the same as what you have with Elements, does no adjustment to the curve.*

Figure 7.47 *The Medium preset boosts contrast slightly and works well with many image types.*

Figure 7.48 *The Strong preset makes a more obvious adjustment when it accentuates shadow detail.*

Black and White Conversions

Did you know that you can do black and white conversions to a raw image? The easiest way is with the Saturation slider. By reducing saturation to -100, you remove all color from the image without throwing away individual color channel information.

To get started, open your image in Camera Raw and reduce saturation to -100, as shown in **Figure 7.49**. The next step is to adjust exposure, shadows, brightness, and contrast. I prefer to use the Alt key (Mac Option) while adjusting exposure and shadows to see where information is beginning to clip, as explained earlier in this chapter.

Figure 7.49 *Reducing Saturation on the Adjust tab to -100 converts your image into a grayscale one.*

Once you have your exposure adjusted, move to the Shadows slider and set the shadow detail level using the same Alt key (Mac Option) preview (**Figure 7.50**).

Figure 7.50 *Use the Shadows slider to adjust the shadow detail, optimizing it for black and white.*

Depending on the adjustments you've made to exposure and shadows, you may or may not need to make an adjustment to brightness, which will control the midtones in your image. I normally find that I need to add a little brightness to my converted images (**Figure 7.51**).

Figure 7.51 *I often boost the brightness a bit in my black-and-white conversions to bring out the highlights.*

The final step in conversion is to adjust contrast. Black and white images often need a boost in contrast compared to the color version of the image. The final image, shown in **Figure 7.52**, includes all the adjustments made to the converted image.

Figure 7.52 *The final adjustment before converting a black and white is to adjust the Contrast.*

Batch Conversions with Camera Raw

The latest version of Camera Raw has added the ability to convert multiple files at once. You can either select the files in Bridge or through the File > Open dialog. Once you have multiple files selected, Camera Raw displays them in a filmstrip along the left side of the converter window (**Figure 7.53**).

Selecting any file updates the Preview area and the settings sliders. When working with images that are all different in their conversion needs, this method can still save a tremendous amount of time by avoiding the need to open each image, perform the edits, open it in Photoshop, and save before moving to the next file.

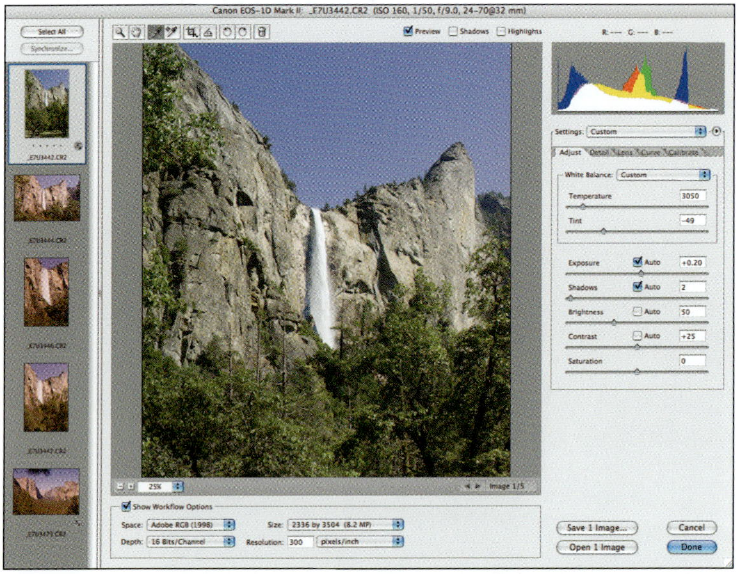

Figure 7.53 *The Photoshop CS2 version of Camera Raw allows you to work with multiple raw files at once, using a filmstrip view.*

Note

You don't have to launch Photoshop to use Camera Raw with CS2. Files can be converted from within Bridge by choosing File > Open in Camera Raw.

Where batch processing really shines, though, is when working with a group of images that all need similar adjustments, such as white balance. It's not uncommon for a studio session to have dozens of images that, when off in color, will all need the same change. Doing this on a file-by-file basis is time consuming, but with the batch feature you can make the change to one file and apply it to all the others with a single click. See **Figure 7.54**.

To begin, select the first image that you want to work on from the filmstrip. Make any changes that will apply to all images, such as white balance or exposure. Now, click on Select All above the film-strip and click Synchronize (**Figure 7.55**). A new dialog box opens with a set of checkboxes for the controls in Camera Raw. You can either select the checkboxes for the settings you want to apply to all images or you can choose one of the settings presets.

Figure 7.54 *You can modify each raw file individually or apply changes to all of them with a single button click.*

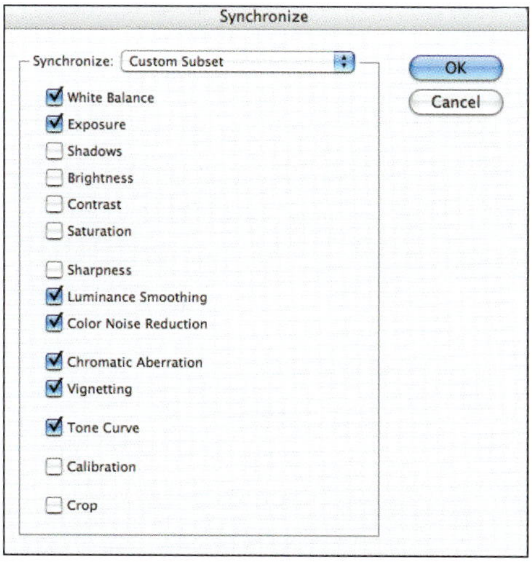

Figure 7.55 *When selecting Synchronize, a dialog box prompts you to select the adjustments you want to apply to the selected images.*

Of course, not every set of files use the same setting changes, but the batch-processing feature in Camera Raw will still save you a significant amount of time. It's very easy to step through your raw files one at a time, making the changes needed to each as you go along. You can move from image to image by either clicking on the thumbnail in the filmstrip or by clicking the navigation arrows below the preview window.

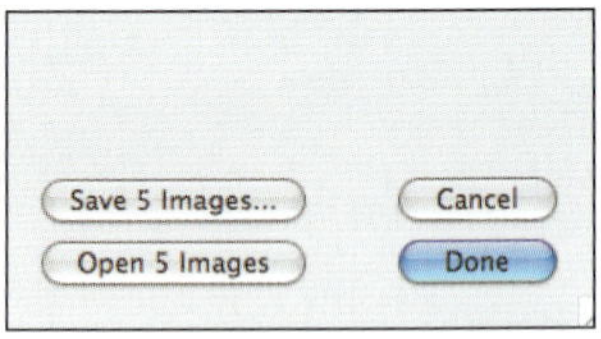

Figure 7.56 *When processing multiple raw images, the Open and Save buttons show you how many files will be processed.*

When you've finished making your edits to all images, you'll see that the Open and Save buttons now indicate how many images will be processed (**Figure 7.56**). When working with a large number of files, it's best to select Save, which will perform all of the requested edits and save your image in the selected format rather than opening all of them in Photoshop. And, if you're converting 20 or 30 images, you'll appreciate that!

An alternate batch method

If you're not using Photoshop CS2, you still have options for converting a number of images. In fact, even if you do use CS2, there are other options. Russell Brown, one of the Photoshop developers, has created a script called Dr. Brown's Image Processor. You can download this from www.russellbrown.com. CS2 users have this script already installed and accessible from within Photoshop from the File > Automate > Image Processor menu, or from Bridge by selecting Tools > Photoshop > Image Processor.

Among the strong points of Dr. Brown's Image Processor are the ability to save in multiple file formats at one time and to embed copyright info into your images (**Figure 7.57**). You can even resize images, making it a handy method of processing multiple images for Web use.

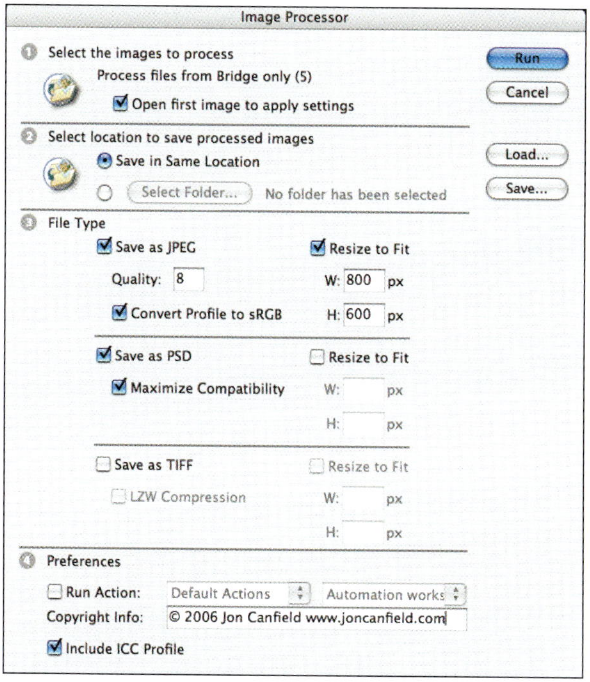

Figure 7.57 *The Image Processor, available in Photoshop and in Bridge, is an excellent tool to convert large numbers of images, especially when you need them in multiple formats such as TIFF and JPEG.*

8 Image Editing

Regardless of your choice in cameras or computer operating systems, you'll be editing your digital images to some degree, even if your only interest is sharing with family and friends or doing basic printing.

For the vast majority of users, this means using Photoshop or Photoshop Elements, both of which are available for Macintosh and Windows. In this chapter, I cover the common editing tasks for tonal correction and color balance that you'll find yourself doing over and over again.

Basic Color Correction

Whether you shoot raw or JPEG, you'll often find that the color balance on your images is not exactly what you were expecting. Unless you use an 18% gray card or the Expo Disc (www.expodisc.com) to set a custom white balance in your camera, a slight color cast in your images is common (**Figure 8.1**). Setting a custom white balance calibrates the camera to the precise color temperature of the light source illuminating the subject.

The image shown in **Figure 8.1**, although captured with the camera white balance preset of Daylight, is a little cool—or slightly blue in tone—due to mixed lighting conditions. When I open the image in Adobe Photoshop Camera Raw, I see that the color temperature is set to 5500K, which is the Daylight setting. By making a slight upward adjustment to 5800K, the cool cast is removed, and the skin tones now have a pleasant and more natural-looking tone, as shown in **Figure 8.2**.

The previous example used a raw image (discussed in Chapter 7) to make the adjustment to color temperature. But what about those times when you shoot JPEG, and what about those images shot before you learned the advantages of raw? For JPEG images, the key

Figure 8.1 *Even when setting a white balance that matches your conditions, it's not uncommon to have slight differences in the color temperature that you can improve.*

Figure 8.2 *After correcting the color balance, the cast in the previous image is easier to detect.*

to correct color balance is matching the camera's white balance to the light source accurately at the time of capture.

A second common problem with color balance is the color cast made by reflections from sources such as water, grass, and so on. These are much more difficult to correct because you'll often find large portions of the photo that look accurate, yet you still need to make adjustments to areas of the image with unwanted color casts caused by the reflections. In cases like this, using Photoshop layer masks on adjustment layers is the best approach to color correction.

Using auto correction

Both Photoshop and Elements offer controls that help with correcting color balance problems automatically. Photoshop CS2 has a single command, Auto Color, that does a scan of your image and attempts to make corrections based on content type. Photoshop Elements, on the other hand, has several auto-correction options that make it easier to fix a number of common problems.

Auto Color in Elements works as it does in Photoshop by scanning the image for color values and making guesses about what tones the colors should have. It's scary how good of a job it can do with this guessing (and at times it's downright hilarious). Additional adjustments in Elements include Auto Color for Skin Tones (**Figure 8.3a**) and Auto Smart Fix, which takes the Auto Color command a step further by also enhancing contrast, levels, and saturation.

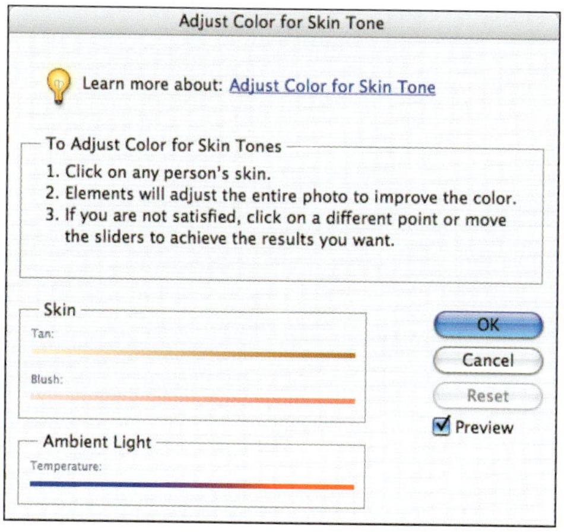

Figure 8.3a *Photoshop Elements has a very useful Auto Color for Skin Tones command.*

Color balance

To correct color manually, Photoshop CS2 features a Color Balance adjustment option. Although this option is not offered in Photoshop Elements 5.0, there is an alternative method that uses the individual color channels within the Levels adjustment layer. As with all image adjustments, it is strongly recommended that you utilize the adjustment layer feature rather than do a regular adjustment, which alters the background layer directly and permanently. By using an adjustment layer, the correction acts as a filter and only changes the appearance of the image and not the original pixels directly. The Color Balance adjustment layer can be found either by clicking the "Create new adjustment layer" button and selecting Color Balance... (**Figure 8.3b**) or from the menu option bar by selecting Layer > New Adjustment Layer > Color Balance (**Figure 8.3c**).

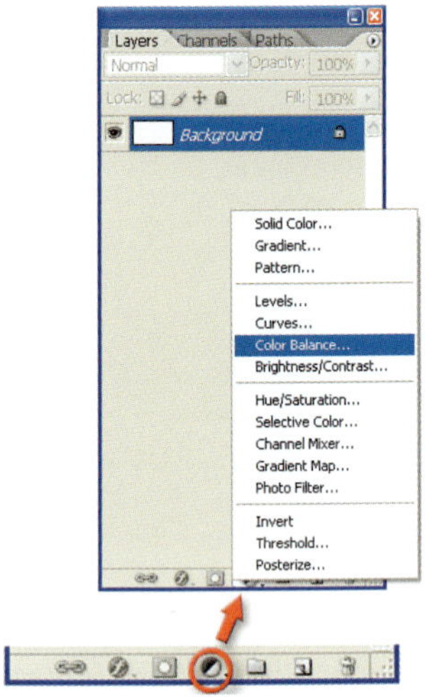

Figure 8.3b *Selecting the Color Balance adjustment layer from the Layers palette.*

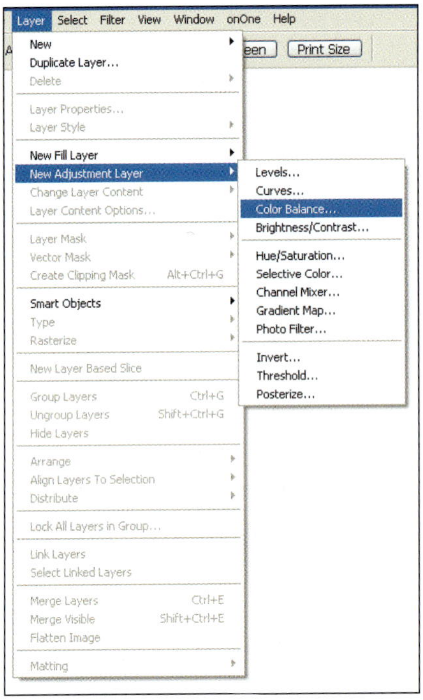

Figure 8.3c *Selecting the Color Balance adjustment layer from the option menu bar.*

The Color Balance dialog box (**Figure 8.3d**) is quite intuitive to use. Three sliders control six primary colors. Each slider controls a pair of complementary, or opposite, colors. Cyan-Red is balanced with the top slider, Magenta-Green with the middle slider, and Yellow–Blue with the bottom. By moving these sliders incrementally, you can adjust and compensate for virtually any undesired color shift. Simply move the slider away from the undesired color and towards its complement. This balances the color and achieves a neutral and accurate tone. In the example, I have corrected for a Cyan-Blue color shift, commonly found in outdoor scenes and landscapes, by adding +26 Red and subtracting -30 Blue.

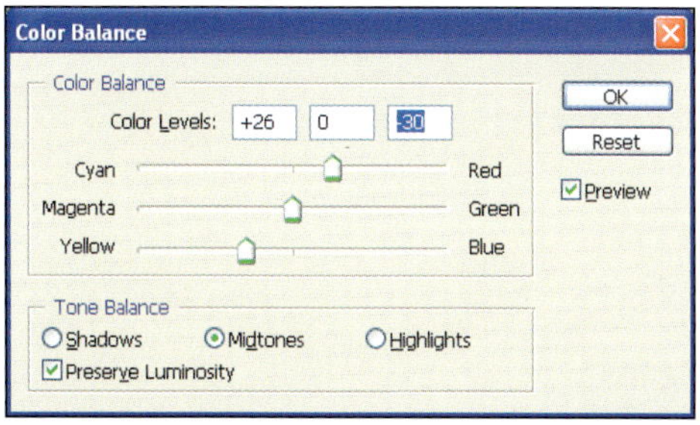

Figure 8.3d *Using Color Balance to correct for a Cyan/Blue color cast.*

In Photoshop Elements 5.0 you can use the Levels adjustment layer to balance the color. In the pull-down window there is a separate option for setting the levels on each of the Red, Green, and Blue channels. Though not as intuitive as the Color Balance sliders, by moving the middle slider on each channel you can effectively modify the image by adding or subtracting that color and its complement.

Color correction is the most challenging aspect of the digital workflow process. A fair amount of practice and experimentation is required to become proficient at accurately determining and correcting a color cast within an image.

Hue and saturation

The human eye loves rich color. If you look at ads in magazines today, you'll see super-saturated color, vibrant hues, and very little subtlety. Is this natural and realistic? Not at all, but because we've become so accustomed to enhanced colors in print media and video, when our eyes see an image that is truly accurate it comes across as flat and unimpressive (**Figure 8.4**).

This is one of the reasons that transparency film such as Fuji Velvia and Kodak E100S were so popular with landscape photographers. You couldn't beat the greens and blues. With those films, the same image in Figure 8.4 looks more like the one shown in **Figure 8.5**.

Figure 8.4 *Although this image is very accurate colorwise, it looks flat because we've become accustomed to seeing saturated images.*

Figure 8.5 *Here's the same image with a saturation boost. Not as realistic, but more pleasing to the eye.*

Digital SLR camera makers understand this need for color, and when you shoot in JPEG you typically get images that have increased saturation. In fact, many people are disappointed when they start shooting in raw because the images look so flat and blah compared to JPEG.

Both Photoshop and Photoshop Elements make it easy for you to increase the saturation in your photos if you want to add some impact by accentuating the colors. Simply choose Layer > New Adjustment Layer > Hue/Saturation (**Figure 8.6**). By moving the Saturation slider to the right, you can increase the vibrancy of all the colors in the image. Use some restraint here, however, because usually any value with the saturation set at a value over +10 starts to make the image look unrealistic.

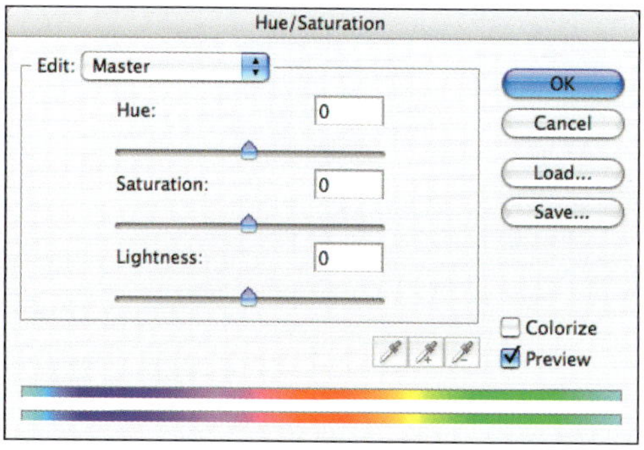

Figure 8.6 *You can modify the saturation in your images with the Hue/Saturation dialog.*

Adjusting Levels

Levels are the basic tool used by Photoshop and Elements to correct shadows, midtones, and highlights in your images. The first stop for a levels adjustment should be the Auto Levels command, found by clicking Image > Adjustments > Auto Levels. **Figures 8.7a** and **8.7b** show before and after views of what Auto Levels can do for your image. You can see a significant improvement in the midtones, as well as some improvement in shadow and highlight detail.

Although Auto Levels can be a great way to adjust your photo, it isn't always the perfect adjustment. You want to go into the Levels control to make your own adjustments for more control, especially as you become more comfortable with image editing. By selecting Layer > New Adjustment Layer > Levels, you see the dialog box shown in **Figure 8.8**.

> **Note**
>
> Throughout this chapter you'll see that I use adjustment layers for almost everything. The reason for this is safety. By making my corrections on adjustment layers, I don't modify the original image, which enables me to go back at any time to make changes if I like.

Figure 8.7a *Before using Auto Levels, this image is lacking detail.*

Figure 8.7b *After Auto Levels the image is much improved.*

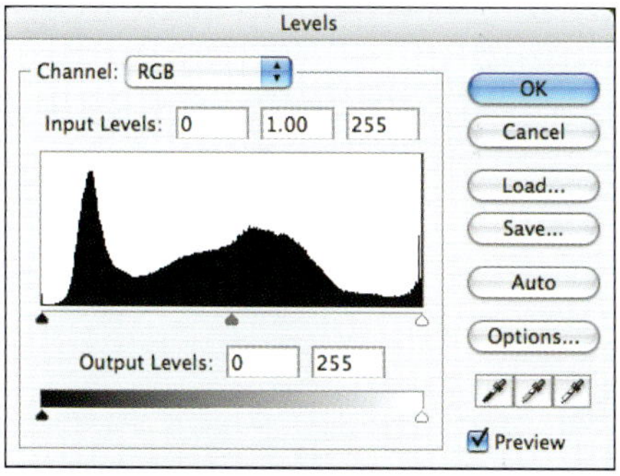

Figure 8.8 *The Levels command lets you control how the image data is seen.*

The Levels control looks very similar to the histogram, the basic bar graph of tonal values, ranging from pure black to pure white, on the combined red, green, and blue channels within your image. Black is on the left, and white on the right. Levels shows two different sets of controls: Input is the upper set of numbers and the ones associated with the histogram, and Output is the lower set of numbers associated with the bar below the histogram. For the time being, we're only worried about the Input levels.

As you can see from **Figure 8.8**, by default the Input levels are set to 0, 1.00, and 255. In other words, black has a value of zero, the gamma (or luminance, or midtones) of the image is 1.00, and white is set to 255. By adjusting any of these numbers, you change what is considered black and white and can adjust the luminance.

Under most circumstances, you want the image data to extend from one end of the chart to the other, maximizing the tonal range in the image. If, as you may frequently find, a photo has the bulk of its data at one end or at the center, the result is an image that doesn't have the full impact that it should. **Figure 8.9** shows an example of this. The original image is underexposed, with most of the data in the lower half of the histogram.

By moving the highlight slider to the right side of the image data, the tonal range of the image is spread out across the entire range, resulting in the photo shown in **Figure 8.10**.

Figure 8.9 *This image is underexposed with much of the image data on the lower end of the histogram.*

Figure 8.10 *After adjusting the highlights there is more detail seen, but the midtones need correction.*

This adjustment has created some exposure problems in the midtones, however, and as you can see in **Figure 8.10** they're a little too light. To correct this, I drag the gamma, or midpoint, slider down to restore some contrast and shadow detail to the image, as shown in **Figure 8.11**.

Figure 8.11 *Adjusting the midtone slider gives the image a final correction.*

Adjusting Contrast

Contrast adjustments can turn a flat-looking photo into something entirely different (**Figures 10.12a** and **10.12b**). Contrast adjustment works by enhancing the edges in your image.

Both Photoshop and Elements have an Auto Contrast setting that often does a very good job of adjusting your image to the right level. Simply select Image > Adjustments > Auto Contrast.

Figure 8.12a *Here's a typical flat image that needs a boost in contrast.*

Figure 8.12b *After choosing Auto Contrast, the image has much better definition.*

Although Auto Contrast works well in many cases, it isn't the perfect solution for every image. That would be way too easy. So, for those times that Auto Contrast doesn't produce the desired result, simply select Edit > Undo Auto Levels (Command+Z on the Mac, Ctrl+Z on Windows) and then select Layer > New Adjustment Layer > Brightness/Contrast to show the dialog in **Figure 8.13**. Moving the Brightness slider to the right increases the overall midtone brightness in the image exactly as the gamma slider does in Levels. Moving the Contrast slider to the right increases the contrast by making the dark tones darker and the light tones lighten in equal increments.

Although this can be a quick fix in many images, the Levels adjustment allows much more control by enabling you to move the Shadow and Highlight sliders independently of one another for a more customized contrast adjustment. In most cases, only a slight highlight increase is warranted to prevent the loss of highlight detail. A heftier increase in the shadows can then be applied without further affecting the highlights.

In summary, Brightness/Contrast can provide quick, wholesale adjustments, but Levels offers the most accurate control.

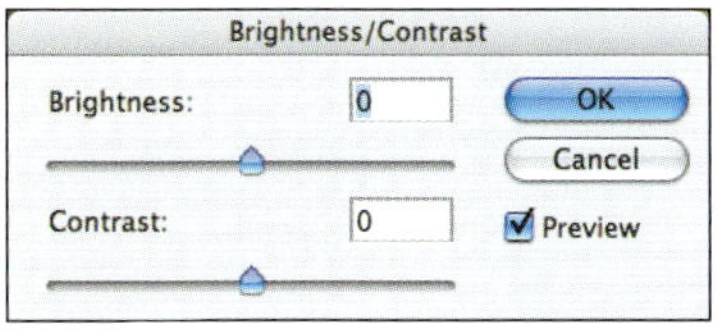

Figure 8.13 *If Auto Contrast doesn't work the way you want, you can choose the Brightness/Contrast command to make the adjustment manually.*

Sharpening Your Images

If there's one thing about editing digital photos that frustrates people, it's how to sharpen them. There are two unwritten truths in digital photography:

- Every digital photo needs to be sharpened.
- Everyone oversharpens their images until they learn how to do it correctly.

Luckily, I'm going to teach you how to get past truth number two.

Unsharp Mask explained

The term Unsharp Mask is often confusing. If you came from a traditional film and darkroom background, you're familiar with the process of masking during development. But for digital photographers, or those who have never spent time in a darkroom, the idea of masking can be hard to grasp. Essentially, in masking you're masking, or hiding, the "unsharp" areas. In digital photography, the job of masking is done by enhancing the contrast between edges in your photo.

Photoshop does this with the Unsharp Mask filter (Filter > Sharpen > Unsharp Mask) (**Figure 8.14**). Other image-editing programs have similar controls, sometimes with different names, but always with the same method of sharpening. With three controls available to define how edges are found and enhanced, you have a great deal of control over the final result. Let's take a closer look at each of the Unsharp Mask controls to understand how they work.

Figure 8.14 *Unsharp Mask is a powerful filter that allows you to improve the appearance of your digital photos. Don't be fooled into thinking it will fix a blurry photo, though.*

- **Amount** controls how strongly the contrast effect is applied to your edges. Essentially, you're increasing the percentage of contrast between pixels to give the appearance of a sharp edge. The sharpening appears in your image as a halo along the edges affected by the filter.
- **Radius** determines the pixel width of the edge that will be affected by the amount of increased contrast. Radius is the most important adjustment of the three controls and can ruin a photo quicker than you can say, "Oops." **Figure 8.15** is an example of what happens when the Radius is set too high. You can see the distinct halo, or glow, around the edges of Devil's Tower. Last time I checked, Steven Spielberg notwithstanding, this wasn't a natural occurrence here. And very few things scream "digital" like an oversharpened image.

Figure 8.15 *Oversharpening a photo adds an unnatural-looking halo around the edges of the image.*

- **Threshold** defines what constitutes an edge by determining how much difference in tonal value is required between adjacent pixels for them to be considered an edge. A low setting of 3 is adequate for most images and means that any adjoining pixels with a difference in tonal value of 3 or more will be considered an edge that will have contrast applied to it for sharpening. A higher setting requires the filter to look for a greater difference in tonal values between adjacent pixels and reduces the number of edges, resulting in less overall sharpening. Threshold values range from 0-255, with 0 requiring no tonal difference (all pixels are edges) and sharpening applied to the entire image. With a setting of 255, no pixels qualify as an edge, and the image receives no sharpening at all.

Now, by themselves these controls aren't hard to understand or master. It's the interaction among them that can lead to hair loss and increased stress. You see, changing Radius affects how strongly Amount appears, and adjusting Threshold can magnify or reduce the effect of both Amount and Radius. Luckily, the controls are presented in the general order of use. You will typically make adjustments to Amount first, to get a rough value for how much sharpening to apply to the photo. Then, by adjusting Radius, you control how prominent that sharpening is. Finally, you can fine tune the results with the Threshold control.

The sharpening process in action

Sharpening differs based on the intended output—including size and media. It makes sense then that you don't want to apply sharpening to your file until all other editing tasks, including resizing, are completed.

In **Figure 8.16**, you see an original image with no sharpening applied. Edges are soft, and detail tends to blur together slightly, giving the entire image the appearance of being a bit out of focus.

Figure 8.16 *Here's the original image prior to sharpening. Edges are soft with a lack of detail throughout.*

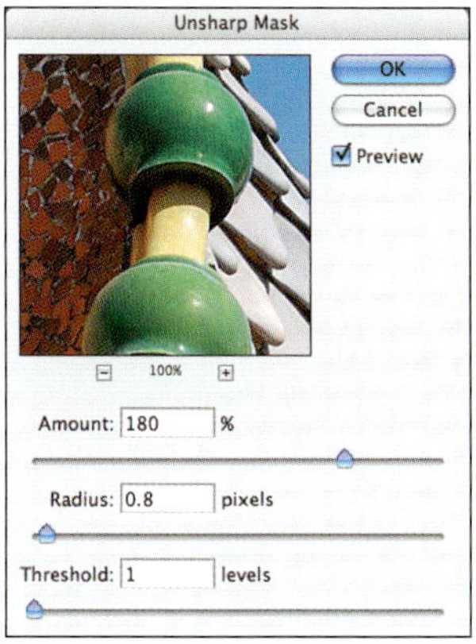

Figure 8.17 *After setting the Amount control, things are looking much better.*

The first step in sharpening this image is to set the Radius to a rough estimate of what I think the image will need. In this case, I've selected a width of .8, which is a good compromise number. A pixel width higher than 1.0 in most images can begin to adversely increase the halo, or glow, around the images' edges. Next, I set the Amount to control how strongly the effect is applied (**Figure 8.17**). In this case, a setting of 180% gives me the look I want without overemphasizing the edges. Finally, I set the Threshold to 1, which prevents lower contrast areas from being affected but still finds the edges of tiles and roof lines to produce the sharpening shown in **Figure 8.18**.

Figure 8.18 *Here I've fine-tuned the sharpening effect with the Threshold slider.*

A few sharpening guidelines

Although every image situation is unique, there are some general guidelines that will help you with using the sharpening tools. I go into these in great detail in my book *Print Like a Pro* (Peachpit Press, 2006), where I have an entire chapter devoted to the magic of sharpening.

- **People are soft.** People don't need to look as sharp as other subjects. Lower Radius and Amount settings are better when doing portraits. Particularly with women and children, you normally want to avoid enhancing contrast in the skin. The only key element that you should be going for is sharpness in the eyes. If your software supports it, select the eyes and sharpen them separately.
- **High detail, low radius.** Highly detailed images work best with low Radius settings in the range of .4 to 1.0, and a higher Amount setting in the 200%–275% range. Keeping the Threshold at a low setting of 0–3 is normally the best choice here.
- **Low detail, high radius.** Images with low detail, or ones that you want to avoid strong edges in, such as portraits, require higher Radius setting, often in the 2–4 range. Conversely, you want to lower the Amount to 75–150% on average to avoid overemphasizing the edges. Increasing the Threshold setting to a range of 7–12 is typical for this type of image.

A Resources

In this appendix, I've compiled a list of companies and products that you should find useful as you begin to explore the world of digital SLR photography and image editing. This list is by no means complete, (that would be a book of its own!), but is a compilation of what I feel are some of the best products in their categories.

Cameras

Canon and Nikon are the two giants in the field, but there are several other quality dSLRs that you may want to look at.

Canon

www.canon.com
1-800-OK-CANON (general information)
1-800-828-4040 (support number)
One Canon Plaza
Lake Success, NY 11042

Canon offers a complete line of cameras, lenses, flashes, and other accessory products as well as photo printers.

Nikon

www.nikonusa.com
1300 Walt Whitman Road
Melville, NY 11747

Nikon has a complete line of cameras, lenses, flashes, and other accessory products and scanners.

Olympus

www.olympusamerica.com
1-888-553-4448
3500 Corporate Parkway
Center Valley, PA 18-34

Olympus is the primary maker of 4/3 camera systems, including a full line of lenses, flashes, memory cards, and photo printers.

Pentax

www.pentax.com
1-800-877-0155
600 12th Street Suite 300
Golden, CO 80401

Pentax has several models of digital SLRs along with a wide line-up of lenses. You'll also find flashes, light meters, and other accessories.

Samsung

www.samsungcamera.com
1-201-902-0347
40 Seaview Drive
Secaucus, NJ 07094

A Pentax by any other name would likely be the Samsung Digimax. Both camera systems offer the same features and accessories.

Sigma

www.sigmaphoto.com
1-800-896-6858
15 Fleetwood Court
Ronkonkoma, NY 11779

Sigma makes the SD series of digital SLRs which use the Foveon sensor (covered in Chapter 1). They also have a complete line of lenses and flash accessories.

Sony

www.sonystyle.com
1-877-865-SONY

A year ago, this would have been Konica-Minolta. That highly respected brand is now marketed by Sony under the Alpha label. A full line-up of lenses, flashes, and accessories are available for the Alpha.

Lenses and Filters

The camera body is just the beginning of your journey in digital SLR photography.

Lensbabies

www.lensbabies.com
1-877-536-7222
516 SE Morrison St. Suite M4
Portland, OR 97214

Possibly the most fun you'll have with a lens on your camera. Lensbabies are available for a variety of camera mounts.

Sigma

www.sigmaphoto.com
1-800-896-6858
15 Fleetwood Court
Ronkonkoma, NY 11779

In addition to cameras, Sigma has a wide range of lenses for different brands of cameras, including Canon, Nikon, and Olympus.

Tamron

www.tamron.com
1-631-858-8400
10 Austin Blvd.
Commack, NY 11725

Tamron has a full line of lenses for Canon, Nikon, Pentax, and Sony (Konica-Minolta).

Tokina

www.thkphoto.com
1-800-421-1141
2360 Mira Mar Ave.
Long Beach, CA 90815

Tokina lenses are available for Canon, Nikon, Pentax, and Sony (Konica-Minolta).

Singh-Ray

www.singh-ray.com
1-800-486-5501
221 SE Highway 31
Arcadia, FL 34266

Far and away the highest quality filters I've ever used. They're pricey, but you can't beat them for optical goodness.

Hoya

www.thkphoto.com
1-800-421-1141
2360 Mira Mar Ave.
Long Beach, CA 90815

Good quality filters at a reasonable price. I'm especially fond of their IR filters.

B+W

www.schneideroptics.com
1-800-228-1254
7701 Haskell Ave.
Van Nuys, CA 91406

Another high-quality line of filters, very popular with pro photographers everywhere.

Tiffen

www.tiffen.com
1-631-273-2500
90 Oser Avenue
Hauppauge, NY 11788

Affordable filters, along with a wide range of special-effects filters.

Accessories

The more you get into photography, the more stuff you seem to need. Here are some good places to get that stuff.

Bogen Manfrotto

www.bogenimaging.us
1-201-818-9500
565 East Crescent Avenue
Ramsey, NJ 07446

A full line-up of camera bags, tripods, lightmeters, flashes, and more.

Kirk Enterprises

www.kirkphoto.com
1-800-626-5074
333 Hoosier Dr.
Angola, IN 46703

Camera accessories, tripods, tripod heads.

Really Right Stuff

www.reallyrightstuff.com
1-888-777-5557
205 Higuera St.
San Luis Obispo, CA 93401

Tripods, tripod heads, mounting plates, and panoramic tools.

Gitzo

www.bogenimaging.us
1-201-818-9500
565 East Crescent Avenue
Ramsey, NJ 07446

High end tripods, including lightweight carbon fiber models.

Velbon

www.velbon-tripod.com
1-973-428-9800
ToCAD America
300 Webro Rd.
Parsippany, NJ 07054

Tripods and tripod heads.

Giotto

www.giottos.com
1-973-808-9010
16 Chapin Road
Pine Brook, NJ 07058

Tripod heads and sensor- and lens-cleaning accessories.

Photographic Solutions

www.photosol.com

Sensor Swab cleaning products.

Visible Dust

www.visibledust.com

The Sensor Brush is my favorite for getting rid of dust from the sensor.

Memory Cards

Oh, you think you got one that'll be big enough. Eventually you'll think again.

Lexar

www.lexar.com
1-510-413-1200
47300 Bayside Parkway
Fremont, CA 94538

Compact Flash, SD, xD, and memory card readers.

SanDisk

www.sandisk.com
1-408-801-1000
601 McCarthy Blvd.
Milpitas, CA 95035

Compact Flash, SD, xD, Memory Stick, and memory card readers.

Kingston Technology

www.kingston.com
1-877-546-4786
17600 Newhope St.
Fountain Valley, CA 92708

Compact Flash, SD, memory card readers, and portable media.

ATP

www.atpinc.com
1-408-732-5000
750 North Mary Ave.
Sunnyvale, CA 94085

Compact Flash, SD, xD, and memory card readers.

Delkin Devices

www.delkin.com
1-800-637-8087
13350 Kirkham Way
Poway, CA 92064

Compact Flash, SD, xD, Memory Stick, card readers, batteries, and LCD shades.

Magazines

Magazines are a terrific way to stay current with everything photographic.

PC Photo

www.pcphotomag.com
1-310-820-1500
Werner Publishing Corporation
12121 Wilshire Blvd., 12th Floor
Los Angeles, CA 90025-1176

One of my favorite general digital photography magazines.

Popular Photography

www.popphoto.com
1-212-767-6000
1633 Broadway
New York, NY 10019

A good all-around magazine covering photography.

Outdoor Photographer

www.outdoorphotographer.com
1-310-820-1500
Werner Publishing Corporation
12121 Wilshire Blvd., 12th Floor
Los Angeles, CA 90025-1176

The best magazine for outdoor photography.

Digital Photo Pro

www.digitalphotopro.com
1-310-820-1500
Werner Publishing Corporation
12121 Wilshire Blvd., 12th Floor
Los Angeles, CA 90025-1176

Geared towards the pro and more advanced shooter.

Shutterbug

www.shutterbug.com
1-321-269-3212
1419 Chaffee Drive Suite 1
Titusville, FL 32780

Excellent coverage of a wide range of photo topics.

American PHOTO

www.popphoto.com/americanphoto
1-212-767-6000
1633 Broadway
New York, NY 10019

Another fine magazine covering a range of photography topics.

Web Sites

Here are a number of Web sites that you'll find interesting and useful. The Web is a very dynamic place, so by the time you read this, some may be gone, and there will certainly be new sites to explore.

www.fredmiranda.com

Photo reviews and a very active community of photographers.

www.photoworkshop.com

Great info on this site, especially for Canon users. Full access requires a subscription.

www.dpreview.com

Very active community of posters, and up-to-date product reviews.

www.photographyblog.com

An English site, with good reviews and updated news.

www.photomigrations.com

Devoted to nature and wildlife photographers, image critiques, forums, and monthly articles.

www.nanpa.org

The home of the North American Nature Photographers Association.

www.microsoft.com/prophoto

Microsoft has several photo related web sites, this one is the best of the bunch and always has topics of interest to a wide variety of people.

www.joncanfield.com

Need I say more? I had to include my own site!

Instruction

Sometimes the fastest way to get the best information is straight from the horse's mouth.

BetterPhoto.com

www.betterphoto.com

Without a doubt, the premier online photography instruction site with lessons on all aspects of digital photography.

Lepp Institute

www.leppinstitute.com

Three- and five-day classroom sessions with some of the top photographers and instructors in the country.

Santa Fe Workshops

www.sfworkshop.com

A wide range of courses on digital and film photography in a beautiful location.

New York Institute of Photography

www.nyip.com

The original correspondence photography school, and still one of the best.

Great American Photography Workshops

www.gapweb.com

Great instructors in some of the most beautiful locations in the country.

B Glossary

AE Auto-exposure.

AF Auto-focus.

ambient light In any scene ambient is natural light.

aperture An opening within the lens that controls how much light reaches the sensor. Apertures come in **f-stops**, such as f/5.6 or f/22. Each successive f-stop, as the number goes up, decreases the light reaching the sensor by half. Aperture also affects **exposure** and **depth of field**. The lower the aperture number, the *faster* the lens.

Aperture Priority mode An automatic mode available in most dSLR cameras in which you choose the aperture and the camera chooses the correct shutter speed.

artifacts Unwelcome visual distortions in an image, such as **blooming, chromatic aberrations, noise,** and **JPEG compression**.

aspect ratio A measurement of the relation between the width and the height of an image. Most digital cameras (along with 35mm cameras) use a 3:2 aspect ratio, though other ratios, such as 4:3 and 16:9, are also found.

blooming When overexposed **pixels** affect neighboring pixels, causing a brightening type of distortion.

brightness The intensity of light shown in an image.

buffer The camera's onboard memory, available for storing images before the data writes to a memory card.

CCD Charge Coupled Device, a type of **sensor** used in **dSLR** cameras. Light enters the camera and strikes the CCD, and the CCD converts the light into a digital image. In a separate part of the camera, the image undergoes digital-to-analog conversion. CCD sensors are generally more expensive than **CMOS** sensors.

CMOS Complementary Metal Oxide Semiconductor, a type of **sensor** used in **dSLR** cameras. Cameras with CMOS sensors are generally less expensive than those with CCD sensors. CMOS works in a similar way to CCD, but does more of the computational work at the sensor, rather than in a different part of the camera.

clipping Image data that is lost due to pushing pixels past their **exposure** limits, such as shadow clipping and highlight clipping.

contrast The gradation of tones from darkest to lightest in an image.

continuous shooting speed How many images per second the camera is capable of capturing.

depth of field The area of an image measured from the nearest point to the camera to the farthest point away that is in focus. A large depth of field, which is determined by the **aperture**, means much, if not all, of the image is in focus; small depth of field means only a certain area of the image is in focus.

depth-of-field preview Closes the aperture down to the selected setting to let you see what areas of your scene will be in focus when you take the picture.

digicam Point-and-shoot digital camera.

DPI Dots per inch, a measurement of inkjet printer **resolution**. The larger the DPI, the higher the resolution of the printed image. Not to be confused with **PPI**, or pixels per inch.

dSLR Digital single-lens reflex, a type of digital camera that is the subject of this book. dSLRs are digital versions of 35mm single-lens reflex cameras, the most popular kind of camera used for professional-quality photography.

exposure The amount of light that the camera allows to reach the sensor, controlled by **aperture** and **shutter speed**.

exposure compensation Used to adjust for dark or bright subjects. Modifies the automatic exposure by adding or subtracting light from the exposure setting.

f-stop A series of preset **apertures**, stated in fractures such as f/5.6 and f/8. As the numbers go up, each f-stop reduces the width of the aperture by half.

focal length Measured in mm (millimeter), the distance from the optical center of the lens to the sensor when the image is "in focus." The shorter the focal length, the larger the field of view.

full-frame sensor An image sensor on a dSLR camera that is the same size as a frame of 35mm film, or 24mm x 36mm.

grayscale An image made up solely of black and white tones.

highlights The lightest pixels in a digital image.

histogram A graph of the distribution of colors in an image, with the colors graphed horizontally (x-axis) and the amount of each color represented on the y-axis.

hue What we usually think of as *color*. A color's hue is that color aspect that makes it different from other colors.

image editor A program, such as Adobe Photoshop or other proprietary ones that come with most cameras, that allows many aspects of a digital image to be edited.

image sensor The digital equivalent of film. A sensor collects the photons that pass through the camera and creates an image of pixels from it.

ISO In film photography, ISO (International Standards Organization) is the rating of the film's speed, such as 100 speed, 400 speed, and so on. The higher the film speed, the more sensitive it is to light, but the grainier the picture will be. dSLR cameras have kept ISO ratings but have applied them to the sensitivity of the sensor. Increasing the ISO setting allows for photography in lower light situations, but again, with grainier results.

JPEG Joint Photographic Experts Group. JPEG is thought of as a file format for digital images, but is more correctly defined as a method of compression in which data is discarded to make the file smaller.

luminance A measure of the intensity of light in an image, arrived at by averaging the lowest **RGB** values and the highest ones.

maximum burst How many images you can capture before the camera pauses to write the images to a memory card.

megapixel One million **pixels**. The more pixels, the higher the potential **resolution** of a camera.

memory card A small card used to store the images captured by your camera. Sony Memory Stick, CompactFlash (CF), Secure Digital (SD), and the xD-Picture Card (xD) are all common memory cards.

midtone A tonal value that lies halfway between an image's **shadows** and its **highlights**.

noise The digital equivalent of grain in film, caused by making the image sensor too sensitive.

PPI Pixels per inch in a digital image. The higher the PPI, the better the image quality. 300 ppi is a very common resolution that produces high-quality prints. Not to be confused with **DPI**.

pan To move the camera sideways to follow a moving object.

photodiode The element in an image sensor that collects the light and converts it into electrons.

photosite The union of a pixel and its color filter on an **image sensor**.

pixel Short for *picture element*. A single point in a digital image that is assigned a specific tone and color. Millions of pixels enable smooth transitions of tone and color to produce accurate renditions of an image. The term also refers to points of light on a monitor screen that make up a digital image.

prime lens A lens with a fixed focal length.

raw An image format in which no processing is done by the camera; a raw image is a recording of the raw light values that hit the sensor.

recycling time The amount of time it takes the flash to prepare for a second image.

resolution The number of pixels in an image measured in **PPI**

RGB Red, green, and blue. Digital-imaging systems, such as digital cameras, use combinations of pixels in these three colors to make all other colors.

saturation A measure of the intensity of color in an image. High saturation means the image has less gray in its tones; low saturation images have a lot of gray.

shadow The darkest parts of an image.

Shutter Priority mode An automatic mode available in most dSLR cameras in which you choose the shutter speed and the camera chooses the correct aperture.

shutter speed The duration that light is allowed to reach the sensor, measured in fractions of a second, such as 1/60. A fast shutter speed means that the shutter, which normally blocks light from reaching the sensor, is opened for a very brief period. Longer shutter speeds leave the shutter open for longer, allowing more light to reach the sensor.

tilt The movement of the front of the camera as it is angled up and down.

white balance A variety of settings that allow the camera to compensate for different sources of light illuminating the scene (daylight, shade, cloudy, twilight, tungsten light, flash, and custom).

zoom lens A lens with an adjustable focal length covering all ranges.

Index

D

J

K

L

M

N